Gardening on Main Street

Gardening

By BUCKNER

Illustrations

on *Main Street*

HOLLINGSWORTH

by Eva Cellini

Rutgers University Press

New Brunswick, New Jersey

For Bill

The New-England Galaxy, Sturbridge, Mass., has kindly
granted permission to reprint three articles by
Buckner Hollingsworth that originally appeared in
that magazine. They are "Spring in New England,"
published in the Spring 1964 issue, here entitled
"Spring"; "Across the Fence," from the Fall 1965
issue; and "When Summer Comes to Town," from the
Summer 1966 issue.

Contents

Gardening on Main Street

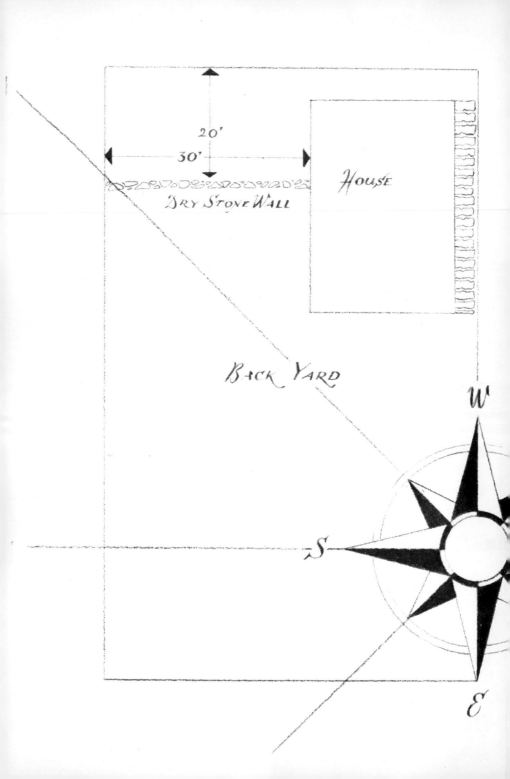

20'

30'

DRY STONE WALL

HOUSE

BACK YARD

W

S

E

Some Posies

No whimsy is intended by the words I have written at the head of this chapter. God forbid! But mine is a New England garden, and in this remote northern section of the Connecticut River valley the word "posy" is used without the slightest self-consciousness as an ordinary part of common speech.

Words, like flowers, are delightful. Like flowers they have color and texture. Like flowers they can evoke the atmosphere of an earlier time. "Posy," for instance, is a word which has heretofore carried for me overtones of the lush sentimentalities that often surrounded flowers in the nineteenth century—artificial as a lace-paper valentine. To hear the word used entirely without affectation as a commonplace noun both entertained and surprised me.

The first time it happened was on a bitterly cold day in March. With my mind full of the gardening that I hoped to begin the following month, I went out into the hall to speak to our plumber. He had just finished doing something delicate and intricate to the intestinal tract of our water system and was shrugging himself into a heavy lumberman's jacket.

We talked of the weather, but he did not share the usual pessimistic attitude of most Vermonters, who tend to anticipate blizzards until well into May. "Five below at my house this morning," he said cheerfully, "but it's bound to break soon." His craggy face broke into a broad, semi-toothless smile—"It'll be good to see the posies again, wun't it," he added—and was on his way.

Since then I have grown accustomed to hearing the word used in casual talk, most often by the older country people. Only a few weeks ago, when scores of regal lilies made a glory of my garden, I heard a very old gentleman say to his wife, "Come, my dear, I am going to take you across the street to see the posies."

"Piny" is another archaic word that crops up from time to time, pronounced in these parts as if referring to a pine tree but actually intended as "peony." Then one morning my husband turned up still another when he told the country neighbor who supplies us with fresh eggs that I was sick in bed. As he took his leave the old man expressed a polite hope that I would soon recover from my "distemper."

Frail threads these, but they lead those of us who enjoy historical associations far back beyond even the earliest settlers in this country—back to Elizabeth's England. "I will make you a bed of roses," wrote Kit Marlowe, "and a thousand fragrant posies."

That first year after we had bought our house on Main Street in a New England village I decided to have a few posies for cut-

ting and as a casual ornament. Real gardening—any gardening—
was the last thought I had in mind. "Our front yard," I wrote
to a friend, "is exactly seventy-six inches deep." Behind that
triumphant, if inaccurate, cry lay twenty-five years of struggle
with eight and a half stony acres in Rockland County, New
York. My inaccuracy was due to the fact that, when writing to
my friend, I defined our front yard as those scant inches that
lay between the house itself and the sidewalk, blithely ignoring
problem areas on either side of the house. To these I shall return
later. But at the moment of writing that letter, those narrow
strips of land on either side of our front door presented an in-
triguing contrast to an experience that must seem familiar to
countless gardeners of the older generation.

When we moved out of New York City to Rockland County
in the early 1930's, our next-door neighbor was a farmer—old
style. Eddie had one horse, one cow, and a flock of goats. He
scratched a meager livelihood from his steeply terraced land
and, thanks to his need of hay, kept our two-acre field well
mowed all summer.

Then there was Old Bill. Bill Stanfield had made his way
north from Virginia, bringing with him unchanged the attitudes
and speech of another time and place. To my husband and me,
two other transplanted Southerners, his manners, his way of
working, and his general personality were as familiar as bacon
and eggs. Old Bill would work three days a week or one—or
even none—but then would turn up just as cheerfully on demand to do the next job. His strong arms swung the scythe that
kept the hillside behind our house free of the encroaching scrub.
He dug my big perennial border—sixty feet long, eight feet
wide, and four feet deep. He taught me how to "take advantage
of" a rock or boulder too big for me to lift when I was building

5

a stone wall or making my rock garden. And out of the goodness of his heart Old Bill gave us a present which was one of the major factors that combined eventually to wreck all the hard work I had put into planting around our house.

I came outdoors one morning to find Bill kneeling a few feet from the lilac bushes. He had scratched a big space of earth bare and on it he was laying a large wreath—tufts of green leaves alternating with spaces where the stems had been pulled off. As I crossed the brick terrace Bill patted earth on the bared stems and sat back on his heels to greet me. "I brung you some honeysuckle," he said. "Tain't none on this place and that ain't right."

In the years to come the Hollingsworths warned their neighbors that if they, the Hollingsworths, were ever found strangled the crime would not have been committed by juvenile delinquents or wandering tramps but by Old Bill's honeysuckle. We escaped, but the lilacs didn't nor did the Roses of Sharon. Once its foothold was established, that honeysuckle wreathed and twined with a speed that the most dedicated gardener could not control.

The honeysuckle took over the more easily because of the war and its aftermath. Old Bill died early in the 1940's and those who might have replaced him were off to the war or to war jobs. Once the war was over they were all off again—off with the bulldozers and other fearsome machines that were sweeping the countryside bare of trees, shrubs, and even of topsoil to make way for the sprouting new "developments."

Eddie too had died, and only with great difficulty and at great expense could we get our big field mowèd once a summer. The lot of the small landowner in the metropolitan area had become hard indeed.

Those last years of struggle in Rockland County had prejudiced me against gardening—I thought forever. But I foresaw no great trouble in growing a few flowers for cutting on the little plot beside the house.

The obvious place to do this planting was on the plot of land on the south side of our house where, eventually, my garden took shape. Entrance to this plot, in those early days after we bought the house, was all but blocked by a huge untidy mock orange, and two others stood in opposite corners. Once that obstructing bush had been well clipped, all these, I decided, could stay where they were. They took up a large amount of space, and in the modest area between them, occupied at the moment by a lusty growth of plantain, I would scratch around and grow a few flowers.

Since, however, in the course of telling this story of my garden, I must of necessity refer to other sections of our small property, it may be just as well to pause here for a brief description of the land with which I have to deal.

Our lot on Main Street is a long rectangle which has about seventy-five feet of street frontage on the west and runs east to a depth of some two hundred feet. The house stands on the northwest corner of the lot facing west, and between it and our northern boundary lies a strip of land no more than five or six feet wide. This boundary is marked by a steep flight of stone steps that lead down to our back yard below.

If from the foot of the steps you swing around behind the house and then turn west along its south side in the direction of the street, you face a handsome dry-stone wall about six or eight feet high, running parallel to the street, from the house to the southern boundary of the land. The bank on which the house is built has been partly cut away here to make way for the wall, which, rising firm and straight, supports the plot of land at street level, on which my garden stands.

To return to street level, you approach this garden plot from our front door by walking along the seventy-six inches between the house and the white picket fence that separates our land from the street. Once inside the plot, its depth from the picket fence to the top of the dry-stone wall opposite is exactly twenty feet; its width, from the house to our southern line, is thirty. This is my garden area. That majestic twenty by thirty feet is exactly right for my size. And there are other advantages. As the land slopes gently from the picket fence to the top of the dry-stone wall drainage is practically perfect. Furthermore the soil, even before lavish applications of bone meal and fertilizer, was good.

"That's the finest crop of plantains in town," remarked the village editor, pausing to greet me across the fence one morning as I stood surveying the site of my future labors. It was early September, and we had owned the place for no more than a month.

I kicked at the thick dark leaves that, with their heavy horizontal veins, grew higher than my ankles.

"If this soil will grow plantains as big as these," I retorted, "it should be able to grow flowers."

"Should indeed," said the editor and betook himself to his office next door.

I should have suspected even then the fate that was overtaking me, but in all innocence I made my simple plans.

A friendly gardener across the river in New Hampshire had promised me an incredibly generous collection of iris and phlox, astilbes and delphiniums, Michaelmas daisies and helenium, not to mention all the hollyhocks I wanted. I would dig a narrow bed along the top of the wall for these perennials; in such fine soil they would practically take care of themselves. Then between them and the fence I would grow a few annuals from seed. There would be no problems involved.

Later in the fall Billy, a high school boy of remarkable efficiency, disposed of the plantains for me, and, in spite of my remarks about the virtues of the soil, I followed in his wake, forking in generous quantities of bone meal and dehydrated manure. Although this is dairy-farming country, what some of us wistfully call "real manure" is a treasure beyond price and practically unobtainable. Long before it has reached the gardener's ideal of well-rotted manure, it has been whisked from the barns out onto the fields, so that most of us have come to depend on the commercial product.

After the end of that first long, beautiful, white Vermont winter, I collected my perennials and put them in. Then I sowed my seed, marking the rows with white string stretched between pegs.

Since in order to see tiny seedlings I must get down on my knees and peer carefully, I had a new experience that first spring. I became very friendly with an earthworm.

I say "an" because I never had the slightest doubt that the one I saw day after day was the same one. He was always lying, dark and pinkish, in exactly the same spot where I had seen him the morning before. Also I say "he" because, while I cannot of course be certain, there was something definitely masculine about his fleshy thickness. He was not handsome, but I remembered Anna Warner's suggestion, in her *Gardening by Myself,* that perhaps to a robin's eye he had his beauty. In any case there he was, and for a few moments each day I shared with one of the humblest and most inarticulate of God's creatures the glory

9

of the spring morning. When eventually he failed to keep our rendezvous I concluded sadly that one of the predatory pigeons living in the eaves under the roof of our house had found him out.

The annuals were a casual and ill-chosen lot, all things I liked but planted without thought as to their size and shape only in order to make a blaze of color—nasturtiums, *Phlox drummondii,* cornflowers, calendulas, love-in-a-mist, and sweet peas designed to climb the fence.

The results astonished me, though they should not have. In that too rich soil foliage flourished madly, and few flowers bothered to show themselves. The only annuals that did well were the two dozen white petunia seedlings that I had bought in flats and had planted, not among the other annuals, but in the poor soil of that seventy-six-inch strip under the front windows of the house. These not only bloomed happily but grew so well that tall stems reached up and twined into the lower slats of the shutters, allowing their white bells to wave against the windows. Those windows, I should probably add, are long narrow ones, close to the floor indoors and not far from the ground outside.

The perennials, including the biennial hollyhocks, were pathetic. Iris sent up only a few leaves and no flowers at all. Hollyhocks and delphiniums never reached a height of more than twelve inches, much less bloomed. Phlox and Michaelmas daisies in their season put out no fine trusses of bloom but a few single flowers here and there. The only thing that flourished in that border along the top of the wall was my least favorite— the helenium, which I privately call the brass-bed flower. The individual sunflowers, about three inches across and growing in dense clusters, were handsome in form and texture but of an uncompromising primary yellow, obviously intent on doing violence to the soft pink of the house.

The explanation was shade. In my careless planning I had given no thought to the elm growing at the foot of that dry-stone wall, its graceful canopy of branches overarching the border I had planted. Nor had I noted that the cut-leaf maple that was so beautiful grew only a short distance away. Then across the plot, in the southwest corner behind one of the mock oranges, grew three hemlocks. The reason I had hardly noticed them is that for the protection of electric and telephone wires they had been so thoroughly clipped that they appeared to the passer-by on the street as simply three bare poles. But if one tilts one's head—as I did regretfully before the summer was over—there are three triangles of the familiar dark green so situated as to throw shade where it will do the most harm. All these trees see to it that between them only the central and forward area of the little plot gets adequate sun, and that only from noon on at midsummer.

Just as I had ignored the liability of shade that first year, so too I failed to anticipate another problem that was to confront me the following spring. This was mud. As I made my way out to inspect my plantings every morning, I beat a path between the front windows of the house and the picket fence. Once it arrived at that untamed plot that was eventually to be my garden, other paths took shape following my movements. These paths were soggy throughout May and, as summer advanced, every rainstorm rendered their condition lamentable. Never a tidy housekeeper, I was continually tracking unsightly blobs of soil indoors.

Yet for all the dismal failure of that first season I was fired by ambition. I had learned some valuable lessons. The old, frustrated longing for a garden was born again. As I surveyed the shambles at the end of that summer, I was aware that, in spite of the difficulties, I had two outstanding assets—the climate and the size of the plot.

The climate was an asset because of my personal metabolism, if that is what caused my trouble. It took a first aid course, during the Second World War, to tell me that the state of collapse into which I subsided periodically during New York summers was nothing fancier than heat exhaustion. Under such circumstances gardening is all but impossible, and Vermont offered a refreshing change. There are hot days here, of course, and I moan about them outrageously, but they are as nothing compared with the relentless heat that envelopes the Middle Atlantic states from the end of May until well into September. People speak of crisp, cold, winter days, but I would celebrate the crisp warmth that makes New England a haven of refuge in summer.

The size of that diminutive plot was the other asset: it was exactly right for me. As I am four feet eleven inches tall, weigh about ninety-six pounds, and was in my middle sixties, a twenty-by-thirty-foot rectangle was just about all I cared to cope with.

Looking over the whole situation at the end of that first summer, I decided that shade could be outwitted. Mud could be conquered. On that ideally small plot, working in perfect weather, the form and color that are the essentials of good gardening might be achieved. Again I was going to have a garden.

2

Privacy, Plan, Color
—and Publicity

It is little less than scandalous to put the word "publicity" in the title of this chapter as if it had anything whatever to do with the three essentials of a good garden—privacy, plan, and color. It most emphatically has not. But it is here because, as the inevitable concomitant of my gardening in full view of Main Street, it gives poignant emphasis to the privacy I lack.

Since circumstances have denied me the garden essential that I value most, publicity has pursued my often ungainly horticultural activities. An old woman in blue jeans, lugging pails of sand or humus, handling fork or spade, kneeling or squatting to weed or cultivate, may be an edifying spectacle, but it is hardly the picture of leisured dignity one would like to present to the neighbors. I can, however, in deference to their sensibilities, spare them the sight of the corncob pipe I so much enjoy smoking when I go indoors.

Yet there are compensations to gardening in public. It is good to know, as I do, that my garden on Main Street has become a village institution. It is quite apparent that it is appreciated and enjoyed by all my neighbors, known and unknown to me. It has, too, put me in touch with all the community activities that have any relationship to gardens and gardening. It has even, quite unjustifiably, promoted me to the status of horticultural expert.

It is the geography of the land on which our house stands that dictates that the only place where I can have a manageable garden is on a small plot beside the house and bordered by Main Street. Our back yard, which at first glance appears to be the ideal place for a garden, consists of about a quarter of an acre of land entirely surrounded by elms and maples. Summer visitors, looking out of one of our east windows, often exclaim, "How lovely! Why don't you have a garden down there?"

The words "down there" furnish part of the answer. The bank that our house is built on is so steep that the first floor, where my husband has an art school, is below the level of the street. Originally the dining room, kitchen, and pantries were on this floor, accessible from above by an inside stairway that we had torn out when we remodelled the house. Today one must go out of doors and down a long steep flight of stone-paved steps in order to get to the school and on down to the back yard below.

This makes the back yard a hopelessly impractical place for a garden—much less for the outdoor summer living room that a good garden can be.

In addition to its impractical location our back yard has a further disadvantage from a gardener's point of view. Shade from the surrounding trees is so pervasive that it limits me to bulbs, ferns, and evergreens.

Yet although the privacy of the back yard is denied me, our back yard is a part of our domestic landscape by no means to be despised. In summer we look out over an expanse of shady green. In winter, as now, I can see from the window beside my work table across a dazzling stretch of white and past some village buildings to where the long high ridge of Dingleton cuts horizontally across the sky. It is visible, now that the trees are leafless, between their vertical trunks. My pleasure in viewing this New Hampshire hillside turns a bit of local patriotism topsy-turvy. Vermonters hereabouts claim that the only virtue in living on the other side of the Connecticut River is that, from there, New Hampshiremen can look across into Vermont.

Besides its aesthetic value, our back yard has proved to be a gold mine from a gardener's point of view. It supplies me bountifully with all the humus that I could possibly want. Year after year the leaves of the elms and maples have fallen and, year after year—for decades it would seem—they have not been raked and burned. I can dig down ten, twelve, sometimes fourteen inches before trowel or spade bites into common earth beneath, reddish in color and of a clay-like consistency. The overlying humus is dark brown and silky soft to one's fingers. Many and many a pailful has been lugged up those long, steep steps to enrich my garden, and, with a little sand added, it makes an ideal potting mixture for house plants.

Many of my village friends and neighbors have charming and colorful back yard gardens in which the gardener may work with impunity in the most disreputable clothes. There, too, she may at times relax and read in peace and at other times may enjoy talking with family and friends over tea or a drink. It is this sort of privacy that my garden on Main Street denies me, and I am frankly envious of those who possess it.

My lack of it has, however, taught me to sympathize with the countless young couples who have moved into modern suburban developments. Like me, though for quite different reasons, they are deprived of the satisfying seclusion that the old-fashioned back yard can almost always offer. I saw their problems all too clearly demonstrated some years ago when our son, Kirk, bought a house in a New Jersey development. Several hundred acres of land had been swept bare of every tree, shrub, and blade of grass. Several hundred houses had been built on this travesty of Mother Earth, each individually pleasant enough, but very dreary *en masse*. Not so much as a strand of wire marked where one man's land met that of his next-door neighbor.

In the first flush of his enthusiasm Kirk set out to remedy matters. He located the exact boundaries of his property and surrounded it with a privet hedge. It was, of course, pathetically inadequate when it was planted and continued so, because he kept it rigorously clipped, knowing that only in this way would it eventually provide the protection he wanted. Long before that could be achieved, he had taken his family back to live in New York.

In those early days in New Jersey, however, Kirk and his wife built a brick-paved terrace at the back of their house and screened it with basket-woven split bamboo. Between the screen and the terrace they left a narrow strip of earth in which they could plant some flowers. Potted plants, set at strategic intervals on the terrace itself, supplemented this arrangement and provided more color. This was an inadequate substitute for a back-yard garden, but since it embodied efforts at privacy, plan, and color it was a step in the right direction.

A plan for a garden is an essential, because a plan is the skeleton which can eventually be clothed with the living flesh of flowers. In a subsequent chapter I shall come to my personal solution of the problems involved, but here, for a moment, it may be a good idea to generalize.

Half the fun of having a garden is planning it. But, for those who feel diffident about their own ability in this line, there are many excellent garden plans published in various magazines that specialize in hints to the householder. Still, in every case, one needs to be very sure indeed that the plan, however neatly mapped out on the page, fits precisely the location, exposure, and drainage that one's own land provides. It rarely does, so before he knows it the prospective gardener finds himself making a change here, another there. Thus step by step, if he is to become a dedicated gardener he discovers that instead of adapting a plan someone else has made he is actually creating his own. There is solid satisfaction in so doing.

When it comes to color, personal preference can have its fling. The plan of a garden has, of necessity, some basic limitations. Its location must be related to the house. It must have an axis on which it can be constructed and it must take into account the geography of the land on which it is to stand. A good deal has already been written about color in the garden, but, when all is said and done, the arrangement and juxtaposition of various tints and shades are dependent on the taste of the gardener himself. He may feel some diffidence about his ability to draw up an adequate plan for his garden, but when it comes to color he knows what he likes and acts accordingly. Or, since women have more experience with color because of their concern with clothes than do men, perhaps I should make my gardener female. She, too, knows what she likes and acts accordingly—sometimes in ways her friends deplore.

It is harder, however, to go wrong with flowers than with fabrics, flowers being the beguiling objects they are. But it can be done. For those who, at the end of a season, feel dissatisfied with the color display of that year and are also puzzled as to why they feel dissatisfaction, there are a number of books on the subject that can offer helpful suggestions. I doubt, though that there are many more useful than Gertrude Jekyll's *Color Schemes in the Flower Garden,* published by Scribner's in 1914 and still obtainable in most libraries which carry a good selection of horticultural titles.

That my own color schemes have, by and large, worked out fairly well is due to fortuitous circumstances. I am no artist, having—as my husband says with some asperity—no brains in my hands. But my college major was history of art and I married an artist, so it is possible I absorbed some knowledge of the basic rules of color without knowing it. On the other hand, of course, I may have merely deluded myself into a state of smug complacency! The reader may judge for himself when he comes to the chapter called "Ballerina in Blue Mink," in which, for better or worse, I tell of my efforts to arrive at pleasing color combinations and contrasts.

This intensely personal aspect of gardening sometimes permits a gifted man or woman to achieve the supreme satisfaction of creating with living material a valid work of art. Few of us ever reach this height, but we can strive toward it with the same serious devotion that an artist brings to the colors he lays on canvas.

To return from this aesthetic aspiration to anything so mundane as publicity is rather like assaulting one's memory of the dignified grandeur of the old Pennsylvania station with a walk through the neon-lit shoddiness that it became before its demolition. But in a New England village publicity is mercifully unrelated to Madison Avenue. It is strictly a home-town affair. In so small a community as this—a village with a population of less than five thousand—much news travels by word of mouth or else by means of the local newspapers, which are devoted almost entirely to community affairs and personal items.

The fact that I was at work making a garden right on Main Street was soon public knowledge, with the result that I, a comparative stranger and newcomer, was invited to join the village garden club and at one time even to serve as a delegate to the annual meeting of the State Federation of Garden Clubs. In this way I discovered how such organizations function from the small village unit up to higher levels.

The club membership consists of a female miscellany that ranges from older women who like to grow a few flowers and enjoy the sociability of the monthly meetings to ambitious younger ones who, now that their children are in school, are eager and willing to learn about gardening. Several members are skillful and devoted gardeners, who have provided me not only with many helpful hints, but also with invaluable information as to how to cope with this rigorous climate.

One of these latter has a small nursery where she specializes in primroses and heather, which she grows from seed acquired from famous seedsmen both in this country and abroad. Her garden is a delight from spring until frost, but when the primroses are in bloom it is pure enchantment. It is no hardship for me to contemplate, literally on my knees, the exquisite precision of the patterns of auriculas and the delicate charm of hose-in-hose, set out as they are in the heady company of "ordinary" primroses—garnet and amethyst, pink, yellow and white, and even an incredible ultramarine blue.

Busy as she is, this gardener takes the time to go to the local school in the remote rural community where she herself grew up and talk to the children about plants. She takes them on walks, identifying the flowers and ferns they see, and sometimes she guides them to places right for planting the seeds of cardinal flowers or gentians with which she provides them.

Several of the speakers who have addressed our garden club have talked about Conservation so that, in addition to what I had already read on the subject, I have learned how it affects our own community. The deplorable condition of the Connecticut River and the spraying of roadside vegetation are lively issues in our own locality and in those adjacent to us.

As an organization the garden club does its bit toward community gardening. The flagpole that stands at the edge of the Congregational Church cemetery has been ringed with tulip bulbs. After the flowers have fallen, annuals are planted. Here, on Memorial Day, the village parade turns in off the street. I find it hard to equate the small contingent of old men at the head of the procession with the fresh-faced boys I knew in France in 1918. Next come middle-aged men, the veterans of Guadalcanal and Iwo Jima, of the Normandy landings, and the Battle of the Bulge. A handful of younger men who served in Korea bring up the end of the military part of the procession— and we try not to look too far into the future. There are boy scouts and girl scouts, Masons, Elks, and Lions. The three shots of the last salute are fired, and the high school bugler plays Taps.

The two narrow borders that flank the path from the street to the Old Constitution House are another matter of concern to the garden club. Here again tulips and annuals are planted, in this case to brighten the short walk tourists must take from their cars to the building. Inside a modest frame structure they may see the setting in which, in 1777, the constitution of the Republic of Vermont was signed. The new nation declared itself independent not only of Great Britain, but also of "all the colonies or states of North America." It was not until 1791 that these stiff-necked Vermonters condescended to abandon their national sovereignty in favor of joining the Federal Union as the fourteenth state.

These, then, are the small concerns of a small garden club in a small New England village. Nor are they mean concerns, since they pay due respect to our historic past and look, though with possibly overoptimistic eyes, toward the future.

In addition to the community activities into which the garden club has brought me, there is the satisfaction, as I have said, of knowing that my garden on Main Street has become a village institution—not to say a village asset. This has been brought home to me by the local newspapers.

Almost every summer a photographer from one or another of these papers turns up with the flattering request that he be allowed to take a picture of my garden. As he makes his preparations to do so, he points out with the utmost tact that the gardener is an indispensable furnishing of the garden. Since I am wax in the hands of anyone who uses superlatives in praise of my tulips, lilies, or morning-glories, I have become resigned to this procedure, regardless of the state of my hair or clothes.

After the publication of one of these photographs I am often stopped on the street or in the supermarket, sometimes by perfect strangers, with requests for information. What, please, is the right time to divide iris? Where can one buy a dwarf apple tree? How can one cope with slugs? On no more solid authority than the latest picture in *The Claremont Daily Eagle, The Valley News,* or *The Times Reporter,* many of my neighbors take it for granted that I know all that is to be known about gardening.

If I can answer such questions readily, I am sometimes rewarded with a gratified "Ayah"—which being interpreted means "Oh, yes" or "Sure." This colloquialism is not pronounced "ahyah," but with the first *a* as long as in *a-b-c*—and is one my husband and I especially enjoy.

Yet for all that I am flattered by this public appreciation of my garden and by the many kind words that have been addressed to me across the fence as I work there, I should be only too happy to exchange my gardening in public for the privacy which I personally consider the most satisfying of the essentials of a good garden.

3

Paths, a Pool,
and an
Apple Tree

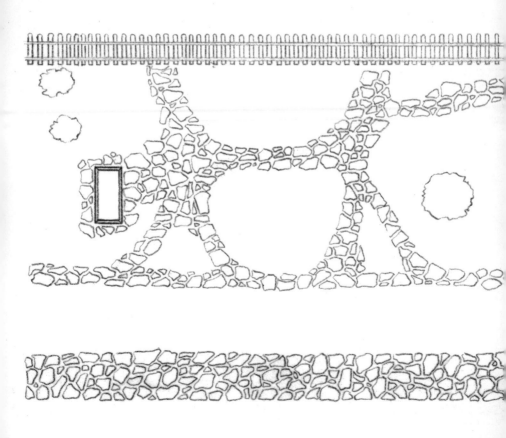

Two absurdly unrelated events toward the end of that first horticulturally disastrous summer occurred to strengthen my determination to have a garden. For the first time in my life I won a raffle, and at the same time a friend modernized her kitchen.

The raffle was held at the flower show put on by our village garden club, and the prize was eight dollars' worth of anything one might choose from the stock of a local nurseryman. I knew exactly what I wanted—a dwarf apple tree. My husband and I selected one that we thought was a beauty and gladly paid an extra four dollars to cover its cost, transportation, planting,

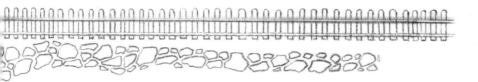

and a year's guarantee. Unfortunately I listened with scant attention to the nurseryman's statement that this was a semi-dwarf. Its subsequent growth, even with rigorous pruning, troubles me, though not yet to the point where I can bring myself to replace it.

Before the little tree could be put in place, that monstrosity of a mock orange near the house had to come out. The mock oranges had proved no less of a disappointment than had the rest of the vegetation that first year. Instead of cascades of dark green leaves foamed over with shining white blooms heavy with honeylike fragrance, only a few oddments of blossoms appeared, each no larger than a quarter and totally lacking the characteristic scent.

I had realized that I should prune and thin the crowded canes of all three of the shrubs in the garden, but I had shirked the herculean task. The bushes could easily have been in place for forty or fifty years and looked as if no one had ever paid the slightest attention to them. The two at the far end of the garden could stay where they were for the time being, but I wanted to get rid of the one to the left of the garden entrance and put the apple tree near where the mock orange had stood.

The same high school boy who had dealt so faithfully with the plantains disposed of the mock orange for me. And I cannot let mention of that heavy chore pass without an admiring word for the way in which he handled it. Anyone who has ever tried to eradicate a well established shrub has some idea of the magnitude of the task, and with each passing year I have realized how splendidly Billy accomplished it. Not once in the four seasons that have passed since then have I found so much as a single sprig of mock orange pushing itself up from some neglected bit of root.

All this took time, and it was in this interval that I was invited to inspect the newly modernized kitchen. It stands in a beautiful brick house, built in 1841, that belongs to friends of ours who live across the river in New Hampshire. We were asked over to dinner one evening, not only to eat one of the superb meals our hostess serves, but also to admire the new setting in which she prepares them.

The new kitchen lived up to every expectation, however extravagant. The electric stove, the huge refrigerator, the well arranged cabinets, the wide, convenient counters, the dishwasher, and a beautiful stainless steel sink were all that any housewife could ask, and I could voice extravagant praise with complete sincerity.

The exhibition over, my hostess and I stepped outside, en route to the terrace for a drink before dinner. And there, lying just beside the kitchen door, was something I had not dared to hope that I would see again—an old fashioned, iron kitchen sink, four feet long no less, and some twenty inches wide.

"What are you going to do with the old sink, Winifred?" I asked.

"I don't know," she answered vaguely, "I think the workmen are going to mix cement in it."

"Oh no they are not," I assured her. "Tell them to bring their own equipment."

Two days later a country boy, who was puzzled by my wanting the rusty antiquity, pulled it out of his truck and carried it into my future garden. I had my pool.

My husband Bill scrubbed off the rust and painted the interior a pleasant blue-green. I dug a hole. Then the two of us eased the sink into the shallow depression and Bill set it true with a level. The first important feature of my garden was in place.

The next, the apple tree, was due to arrive the following week. The situations for pool and apple tree had not been casually chosen but were part of a carefully laid plan. If you stand on the sidewalk outside my garden and draw an imaginary line through the exact center from the picket fence to the top of the dry-stone wall opposite, two of my major garden ornaments have been placed equidistant from this line. The pool, its long side running parallel to the south side of the house, is eight feet to the right of this line; the apple tree eight feet to the left. The tree would have height and curly edges; the pool lies level with the land and has straight lines; but if the proportions of pool and tree are right and they are set with precision they would balance each other. That, at least, was my original idea and I still maintain that it was a good one. But with the years the tree has grown too big. The pool, with ferns and other plants around it, looks too small. Like so many optimists I failed to look far enough ahead.

My miniature garden was to be a formal one. The word all too readily suggests a picture of wide gravelled paths, box-edged borders, softly splashing fountains, stately ornamental statues, and a general decorous rigidity. One need not go back to the eighteenth century to have a formal garden. In fact any garden worth its bone meal is formal. Call the basic idea a plan, pattern, or design—what you will—the garden must have form and is therefore formal. The smaller the garden the greater the need for form and symmetry. Once the basic idea is clearly established in mind, or better still on paper, the details should conform— form again—to it.

Garden and household magazines are filled with garden plans, many of which are excellent, but I have always found it more fun to make my own on the basis of the simple formula that Mrs. Francis King advised country housewives to use nearly forty years ago.

In *The Beginner's Garden* she suggests that the housewife stand in the doorway through which she plans to enter her prospective garden. She should then draw an imaginary line from the exact center of that doorway either to an imaginary point or to whatever object, fence, arbor, or whatnot, where she wants her garden to end. This line is the garden's axis—as important for its existence as the equator is to the earth's geography.

From this simple beginning one can go on to define the outer edges of the garden at equal distances from the axis, and then, the general size and shape clear in one's mind, the details can be filled in. These of course should balance each other.

Thanks to the fact that there is no door in our house from which to step directly out into the garden, I was unable to follow this wise advice literally. However, what Mrs. King was saying is that the axis of a garden is the line along which one naturally views it. My garden is of necessity best seen from the street. This makes the axis run across the width of the garden rather than, after the fashion of most gardens, along its length. But no matter. The axis is there and the garden has been planned around it.

The next step is what an artist would call "pulling the design into shape," and since I am married to an artist the phrase has a familiar ring to me. It means nothing more complicated than working out the details to make a coherent whole. Landscaping a large property is another matter, but a garden—*the* garden —must be a single unit. I worked out the details I wanted and then pulled the design into shape by the same simple expedient with which I also solved the mud problem—paths.

Just as paths were the obvious solution to the mud problem,

so flagstones seemed the obvious material with which to make them. My husband and I drove to a nearby hamlet and invested in half a dozen to start with, figuring that the trunk of our car would carry no more. My request that each flag be broken into five or six pieces brought a reproachful look into the eyes of the workman, who hated to see his beautiful stones so mutilated. But he complied, and we brought a good load home.

The first path laid between the house and the picket fence and leading to the garden was a surprise to both of us. It looked strangely wrong. The flagstones were blue grey in color and seemed bluer against the pink of our house. The stones were smooth, too smooth, and looked alien in front of a house that fitted so perfectly into its austere New England background. Not that flagstones cannot be useful and handsome in many situations, but they looked out of place between those clapboard walls and that white picket fence.

"Ordinary native stone is what we want," said my husband, and ordinary native stone was what we eventually acquired, though not without effort. A friend tipped us off as to how to get it.

"Go back into the hills," she told us. "The farmers are letting their walls go to rack and ruin. Sometimes they even bulldoze them under. Find a good one and then help yourselves. That's what Louis and I did."

My friend is native to this part of the world, but we are outlanders, so we played safe. We drove back into the foothills of Mt. Ascutney and sought out a farmer who obligingly directed us to a wall convenient to the road where we could take away all the stones we could carry. Day after day we came back and loaded up the car.

Vermont is rich in a type of stone far different from the

roughly rounded granite boulders with which I had worked in Rockland County, New York. The Vermont stones are flat on two sides, most often about three inches thick and irregular in shape. They were made in heaven for the laying of paths. Their final virtue is that, thanks to size and shape, they are easily handled, and we collected ours without undue toil. It was October, and the country was ablaze with reds and yellows, pinks and oranges, so that the hillsides flickered as if with flame.

It turned out, however, when I had laid many feet of paths, that there were not quite enough stones to finish the job. It was by then late in the fall and too cold to go stone gathering, so I dismissed the matter until the following spring. Then when our son drove up with his wife and little boy he offered to help me collect the rest of the stones I needed.

We did not go back to our farmer's wall but followed one of Vermont's swift rocky streams that empties into the Connecticut River. At the entrance to an old wood road Kirk turned his station wagon in and drew up on a bank a little above the stream. I wandered about looking at the early spring herbage underfoot, leaving the two males to cope with the rocks, although six-year-old John displayed more enthusiasm than efficiency.

That single carload answered my need, and the paths were finally all well and duly laid.

In the not too distant future I foresee a new time-and-labor-saving device for gardeners. It will of course be made of plastic and will be obtainable either by the yard or in one-hundred-foot rolls, eighteen, twenty-four, and perhaps even thirty-six inches wide. On its surface will be depicted a naturalistic (?) representation of rocks laid in concrete. You will unroll this substance over the proper areas, peg it down with some gadget supplied for the purpose, and then plant sweet alyssum along the edges. As I look at my paths now, it is a satisfaction to know that they were constructed with no shoddy makeshift. They will easily outlast me. They look as if they belonged to the land on which they lie—as indeed they do—and they have for me the additional advantage of evoking pleasant memories.

In laying the paths that would define the pattern of my garden, I worked according to a plan that was suggested partly by the size and shape of the garden, partly by the paths already beaten out during the previous summer. The design that emerged appears on the accompanying sketch.

It is usual but not inevitable for the axis of a garden to be emphasized by a path running along its length. Mrs. King's farm woman might want to step into her garden from her kitchen and would visualize an imaginary line running from the middle of the kitchen door to, say, that small dogwood tree or flat granite boulder directly in its path, fifty, seventy-five, possibly even a hundred feet away. A central path would naturally follow the axis in such a case.

In my garden, however, a central path would be an absurdity. It would have to start against the obstruction of the fence and run across the narrow width of the plot to the top of the drystone wall that drops off into space. Furthermore such a path would carry one's eye far too quickly through the middle of the garden without drawing attention to the larger areas on either side of the axis. A shallow semicircle, set with its flat side against the fence and a second and chunkier semicircle directly opposite permit curving paths not only to define these beds, but also to direct the viewer's attention to the right and left of an axis too short to capture his interest. Yet the axis is there as the backbone of the garden.

A professional landscape architect would probably have

worked out a much better plan than mine. But there is a still further difference between us. He would have drawn his plan consciously aware of certain principles of design. I never put my plan on paper but worked it out on the land itself. I kept that central imagined axis fixed in my mind, but, aside from that, the plan took shape as this or that arrangement seemed right to me and to my husband, on whose sense of design I relied. This is a very amateurish way to work and was only feasible because the area I dealt with was so small. But barring some minor flaws in measurement that I seemed unable to avoid, we have found the result satisfactory.

With the apple tree and the pool in place, and the paths defining the beds laid, the skeleton of my garden was complete. In the summer to come it could be clothed with the flesh and color of flowers.

4

Ballerina in Blue Mink

Ballerina in Blue Mink is as sprightly and gay as the name suggests and represents the most dazzling success with color in my garden. That first summer, after all the paths were laid and the pool and the apple tree in place, I planted three or four dozen seedlings of the petunia Ballerina in the semicircle against the fence and drew a line of ageratum Blue Mink around its curving edge. The petunia is almost exactly the same pink as our house, except that the flowers carry the indefinable glow of living things. The plants sprawl over the ground with lush abandon, thickly covered with flowers. Blue Mink is, in my opinion, the most satisfactory of ageratums—each plant like a well rounded miniature shrub, its fuzzy cushions of bloom well in evidence. In this color scheme I have tried for my ideal of massed color with a good contrast; the number of pedestrians who stop to look suggests that others beside myself find this combination of color satisfactory.

Choice of color is an essential part of planning a good garden. When the design of a garden is well proportioned and well balanced, when blocks of color make good contrasts or blend well together, then the garden has not only charm but may also have grace and even elegance. My own garden has charm but I lay no claim to the more lofty virtues.

Good color in the garden is easier to come by today than it was a couple of generations ago. Then all but a very few annuals could be bought only in packets of mixed colors. Now one has only to look at the catalogues to realize how many gardeners must be following the excellent practice of planting in blocks of color. Asters, pinks, larkspurs, cornflowers, calendulas, petunias, snapdragons, marigolds, and zinnias, to name only a few, can all be bought today in separate colors or shades of color.

Take zinnias, for instance. Whether the space is to be filled by California Giants or the small pompons, a mixture of colors only presents a clash of discord—scarlet-screaming at the dim but persistent magenta, primary yellow snarling at ruby red, and pinks and cream whites lost in the fracas. Yet, properly handled in blocks of color, even that cold, dull magenta can be handsome. I once saw magenta pompons planted in the bay of a terrace with a low-growing silver Artemisia in front of them. Given the other more manageable colors, the possibilities are endless, and I for one am always saddened or irritated, depending on my disposition at the moment, by the waste of time and energy that has gone into producing that discord of ill-assorted colors that mixed seeds yield.

My own garden is so small that, while I dream in blocks of color, I have to admit that the result can be more aptly described as spots of color. These, however, I have tried to balance with each other, and I have tried to make what contrasts I have used sharp and clear.

There are for example those two little triangular beds. They are so small that a single large plant of astilbe, or goatsbeard if you prefer, fills the base of each of the beds to the left and the right of the central semicircle. At midsummer, when the plumes of creamy pink lift above the leaves, the two or three Browallias planted in front of them are spangled with their deep warm blue flowers and, at the tip of the triangle near the apple tree, a cluster of fairy lilies rise crocuslike, much the same color as the astilbe but deeper in shade. These pinks and the strong blue make their appearance on either side of the central semicircle when the gold-throated regal lilies are in bloom. Few would quarrel with the effect.

To my surprise and pleasure my ambitious plans for that small semicircle exceeded my expectations. I had hardly dared to hope that roses, lilies, and peonies would all do well there.

The roses were three floribundas, Fashion, set in a triangle in the front center of the bed between the peonies, with regal lilies filling the curved space behind them.

In June the floribundas did all that any gardener could ask of roses—and what more could any gardener ask? Floribundas are advertised as "everblooming," but I have found this to be inexact. These roses have a rhythm of bloom all their own—or at least mine had. Throughout June the plants were a glory of pink. Then the flowers gradually died away until late in July, when they returned to join the final bloom of the lilies. After another short rest they were back again towards the end of August, and some bloom lingered on even when early frosts cut down many flowers in September.

Roses however, as everyone knows, are prone to bugs, so when I could no longer see well enough to cope with the pests, I passed my plants along to friends, who, I am glad to say, continue to give good reports of them.

I have tried a number of experiments to fill the space once occupied by the floribundas and came nearest to satisfaction last summer when I planted petunias and pansies. The petunia was new to me, Moonstone, a small flower of so pale a chartreuse as to seem almost a cream white. The pansies, planted in front of Moonstone, were steel blue. The only difficulty, however, is that pansies, so trim and neat when you plant them, rapidly grow lax and leggy. I rather think that next year I shall fill this space with white and steel-blue pansies when they are at their peak and then discard them in favor of dwarf sweet peas.

This will also be an experiment, since I have never even seen dwarf sweet peas, much less raised them. I shall have to grow them myself from seed and can only get this in a mixture of colors, but, inconsistent or not, this will not bother me. The mingling of soft pinks and yellows and lavenders, with an occasional splash of crimson or purple, should be charming. It is the scarlets and oranges that make trouble, though even these, handled skillfully, can be stunning.

The two peonies that flank the space where I hope that sweet peas will flourish lack only one virtue—staying power. The time when their breath-taking beauty is on display seems so short. Mine are single Japanese peonies—wide shallow bowls of creamy white with a tight, intricate pattern of pistils and stamens at the center, orange for one of the plants, the palest of lemon yellows for the other. The latter, Sunkist, is my special love, and I wish I had bought its twin instead of the slightly different Mildred Atwood. I could, of course, still buy another Sunkist, but it would be several years before the new plant reached the proportions of the one now so well established; like most gardening grandmothers I take time into account.

Nothing so grand as roses, lilies, and peonies brighten the long, narrow border at the back of the garden, where the shade is dense, but by dint of hard work I have managed to get some color there. Spectacular it will never be; still, through trial and error, I have learned to make it presentable.

After the collapse of all the standard perennials that first summer, I swung to an extreme expedient for that border. It sounded fine. I would plant an evergreen hedge along the top of the stone wall and put lilies in front of it. A host of magazine articles assured me that lilies prefer shade to sun—or could it have been that optimism and desire ignored certain cautious qualifications?

With young Billy to help I drove to some nearby woods

where, with the owner's permission, we collected a dozen sturdy little hemlocks about three feet high. What the roots of these would do to the dry-stone wall along whose top they were to be planted I brushed aside as a problem for the remote future. I was feeling rather desperate and in a sort of *après moi la déluge* mood—reprehensible no doubt, but perhaps understandable under the circumstances.

Any pricks of conscience that might have accrued from this reckless performance were spared me. The little trees, planted in the fall, all died the following summer. And the lilies emulated them. I had bought a variety of mixtures, planning to choose from among those that did well the ones I liked best, then buy more of these and discard the rest. Choice was denied me, however, for not a single bulb of *auratum, regale,* or the hybrids Olympic, Mid Century, and Fiesta produced a flower. Only the two bulbs of *speciosum* sent up stems strong enough to unfurl their Turk's caps, one an exquisite all-white, the other the familiar spotted pink.

Columbines seem to have no objection to it whatever, so it is on columbines that I depend for color in that border during June. Mine are planted in the front and center of the bed, where they get a little sun each day, but they never grow shoulder-high, as do the plants in a friend's garden, which has sun throughout the daylight hours. But even though my plants are small they shake out quantities of bloom and swing their lovely, long-spurred flowers to the delight of all who see them.

Most daylilies, it is claimed, do well in shade. Mine were planted in recollection of the sheets of color that brighten our country roadsides, where the old garden escape has made itself at home. Almost needless to say, nothing like that happened. I put clumps of daylilies at each far end of the border: Lustrous, a good pink; Linda, a delightful ruffled apricot; and Skylark, the palest of yellows, with a golden star in its throat. The plants all flourished and all bloomed, but without the abundance for which I had hoped.

Two other daylilies, Pink Glory and Another Song, were planted in the center of the bed, and there where they got a little sun they did better. Pink Glory, a tall-stemmed, handsome flower, is planted in the exact center of the bed with clumps of Another Song on either side. The latter is by far the best of the daylilies for my garden—not so beautiful as Skylark or Linda, but of lower growth, which makes its proportion right; and the color is the same as that of our house—that ever persistent factor!—only in a much deeper shade.

Since even at their best daylilies provide me with only a scant amount of color I count, from midsummer on, on three annuals, Impatiens, Browallias, and Cleome. If these will flower, as they all do in my back border, I can assure any gardener that they can be depended on in a shady place.

In fact I have come to believe that Impatiens will flourish and flower if planted in wet cement! It comes, of course, in a wide variety of hot and cold pinks and reds, and I like to separate the plants according to these categories. I tend to discard the cold pinks and magentas, not because I do not like them, but because the warm ones go better with the daylilies and give richness and depth to the whole bed.

Here in Vermont the plant is usually called "Patience." "Impatience," which it is more rarely called, is a perfectly good translation of the botanical name, but perhaps Patience is preferred because of an unconscious desire to associate a pretty flower with a virtue. Those who are less sentimental appreciate the fact that there is real impatience in the way the plant snaps its seed from the pod at a touch, just as does our native jewel-weed, to which it is closely related.

Browallia is unfortunate in not having any sort of common name, appropriate or inappropriate. *Browallia.* It would be hard to find a more unattractive collection of syllables. It seems a pity to have to apply them to so pretty a plant and a flower of so rare a color. I found the name not only awkward but hard to remember until I learned the story of its origin, and now it is firmly fixed in my mind.

The three different botanical names that Linnaeus bestowed upon the plant in succession suggest a story whose details it might be entertaining to know. When this new introduction from South America or the Caribbean reached him, in 1735, the founder of modern systematic botany named it *Browallia elata* in honor of John Browall, Bishop of Abo in Finland. Browall was an amateur botanist and an admirer of Linnaeus, whose radical new theories the bishop had defended with vigor.

Something must have happened, for at a later date Linnaeus changed the name—and then changed it again. Bailey's *Cyclopedia of Horticulture* gives the bare bones of the story as indicated by these changes. "In the names of the early species, Linnaeus commemorated the course of his acquaintanceship with Browall: *elata* reflecting the exhalted character of their early intimacy; *demissa* ["weak" or "low"] its rupture; and *alienata* the permanent estrangement of the two men."

Whatever the cause of this shadowy quarrel, now more than two centuries in the past, the very animosity that lives in the Latin words may help others, as it has helped me, to remember the rather difficult name of this prepossessing and useful plant.

The flowers of Browallia—for those who do not happen to know them—are a rich deep blue, warmed only by the faintest tinge of purple. It is so nearly a true blue that one cannot quarrel with its being so described in catalogues, although these, as all canny gardeners know, use the word with such deliberate lack of discrimination that even the "Elks purple" of the annual larkspur is described as "blue"—without quotation marks.

Browallias planted on either side of a group of Impatiens make a very fine show even in my shady border.

Spider-flower, or Cleome, to give it its proper name (which sounds Greek but isn't), performed for me in the most surprising fashion. I had never so much as seen the plant when I picked up a little flat of seedlings one spring day. When my garden books informed me that the plants grew five and six feet high, it was obvious there was no place to put them but at the very back of the long border. I consigned the little things to this unpromising location, expecting nothing. No one was more surprised than I when mighty plants appeared there. By August the whole garden had a backdrop of lush dark green, topped with thickly rounded heads of pink and white flowers from which protruded long pink stamens tipped with old-gold anthers. The flowers abound until frost cuts them down. Like Ballerina in Blue Mink, I now count on replacing them each year as a permanent part of my garden scene.

Color in my garden is not confined to the two semicircles and the long back border, but these provide the color notes that set the key for all the rest. The small areas around the apple tree and between the pool and the picket fence are planted with Ajuga, whose chubby short spikes of blue flowers look well when the tulips are in bloom and whose flat rosettes of bronze foliage are attractive all summer. Running parallel with the pool and between it and the white pine hedge which marks our southern boundary, is a planting of the narrow-leaved Hosta, put there less for the lavender flowers that appear in August than for the fountains of light green foliage that are a pleasant contrast to the evergreens behind them. Neither of these plants is spectacular, but they serve to round out and emphasize more colorful spots in the garden—a job they do with grace and dignity.

Color, as an essential of a good garden, is rarely the static thing that a plan can be. The more devoted to his vocation a gardener becomes, the more certain he is that next year's color will be better than that of the past season. He combs the catalogues in winter; when spring comes he explores the local nurseries. And during the summer he is unable to view flower shows and garden tours with objective eyes. He is always on the lookout for that ideal plant, neither too low nor too tall whose flowers sport a color that he needs or wants. Color is the garden essential that keeps the gardener on his toes.

5

Those Seventy-Six Inches

Those seventy-six inches in front of the house about which I had boasted so happily when we first bought our place on Main Street turned out to be the last bit of our land that received my attention. In the first fine flush of gardening enthusiasm I hardly noticed the narrow strip between the house and the fence over which I had to pass as I went to and fro. It was not until an unsightly mass of crab grass and sorrel sprouted vigorously that I realized something drastic had to be done. God forbid that I should describe this situation as presenting me with a "project" or, even more deplorably, with a "challenge." Like most projects and challenges it proved to be no more than an honest problem—and a minor one at that. But I had ignored it for so long that it took time and trouble before I found a solution. Once found, however, I discovered that I had acquired in that tiny area two displays more dramatic and more spectacular than anything the garden proper had to offer.

Parenthetically I also discovered when I came to deal with that crab grass and sorrel that I had more interest in the latter than animosity towards it. I had never before seen a very dwarf sorrel with mink-brown foliage. The midget plants that spread so lustily in every direction inspired me with less ferocity towards them than regret that they had to go. My weakness for weeds is a handicap that, as a conscientious gardener, I strive to overcome.

During the first few weeks after we bought our house I was far too busy indoors to give any thought to the land around it. But, as a gesture toward a continuity of gardening with which other gardeners will sympathize, I did dig in near the fence some narcissus bulbs which I had brought along from the Rockland County place. "Dig in" is the right phrase, because they were planted so hastily and carelessly that they have never given me much bloom, but they serve to remind me of their pleasant story.

Years ago, when we moved out of New York to Rockland County various gardening friends warned me against "bargains" advertised on the garden pages of newspapers. But in that fall of 1931 Bloomingdale's was offering a collection of one hundred narcissus bulbs for one dollar, and I could not resist so small a gamble. It turned out that the transaction could hardly be classed even as a gamble, for when the package of bulbs reached me it contained, not one hundred, but one hundred sixty-odd.

Originally these narcissus were planted in the bays between a long line of shrubs, but, as so often happens with me, I made too little allowance for the growth of the shrubs. The narcissus bloomed when the canes were bare, but in a year or so their ripening foliage was all but smothered by the overarching green. Heaving a vast sigh for the labor involved—for the bulbs had multiplied prodigiously—I dug them all up and transplanted them onto a steep bank just outside our living room windows— the last slope of our local miniature mountain, known as High Tor.

The following spring, when I rose in the morning I carried my clothes into the living room and counted my blessings out-side the window as I dressed. For several years I enjoyed this diversion until its mathematical aspect was superseded by the sheer delight of having too many flowers to count. I had quite simply achieved a host of golden daffodils. These were succeeded by a host of poet's narcissus with their shining white petals and shallow, yellow red-edged cups. No one had ever ignored well meant advice so advantageously.

Apart from the narcissus bulbs the only attention I paid to the little strips of land on each side of our front door in those early years was to provide them with paths. One of these, the path leading from the house to the garden, was purely utilitarian. It protected my feet from mud as I went to and fro. An exactly similar path was laid to the north side of the house in the interest of symmetry. This path led to nothing more definitive than the white lilac which I eventually planted there to round off that end of the little strip.

These paths bisect the inches between the house and the fence, and it is now time to point out that these inches are not seventy-six but a munificent fifty-eight. The other eighteen lie outside the fence between it and the public sidewalk. They can be ignored here since their final incarnation will be discussed in the next chapter. Thus we are concerned now with no more than the four little strips of land lying on each side of the two paths between the house and the fence.

My first idea for planting under the windows was so successful that I have never changed it. No more than two dozen white petunias, one dozen on each side, do all that any gardener could ask. The bright green of the small seedlings I plant on or just after Memorial Day attracts the eye away from the fading foliage of the bulbs that have gone before. Then, their foothold established, the plants spread and sprawl, filling every inch of the space. The white flowers are not only pretty against the pink of the house but are so abundant that there are always plenty for me to carry in to my horizon-blue living room.

To provide for spring bloom before the petunias could take over, I first put in some tulips, which proved to be as odd a mixture of success and failure as they were of kind.

The successful part of that planting and one that is still a feature of my spring display consisted of two circles of white lily-flowered tulips planted between the living room and dining room windows. Stretching to left and right of each circle that first year I put in a stiff single row of alternating dark red and white tulips, which I took to be Darwins. Given the source of these tulips, I should have known better than to take anything for granted.

After my happy experience with the Bloomingdale bargain, it may ill befit me to criticize any source of supply, but years of experience since then have taught me that it is inadvisable to buy garden material from anyone except from established seedsmen and nurserymen whose products are reliable and whose nomenclature can be depended upon. This I knew quite well, but in the case of those first tulips I succumbed to some gaudy pictures in one of those mail-order catalogues that offer not only bulbs for sale but gadgets of every conceivable description, from an electric toothbrush to a musical garbage can. I was not, then, too surprised when only about half the bulbs I took to be Darwin produced flowers the second year. By the third all but one or two were gone. The lily-flowered variety, bought from the same source, must have been of tougher or better stock, for it still serves me well.

The failure of so many of those first tulips would be hardly worth mention were it not for the pleasure that three of them gave me before they disappeared. Two of these were the so-called Candelabra tulips, which I had ordered separately and which I had planted at some distance from the others. The bulbs are said to be short-lived, so their single season of bloom was perhaps not surprising. Even so they are worth the time and trouble involved. Mine did not rise to the great height attained by the lily-flowered type, but the short, sturdy stem branches out, producing four or five flowers to a bulb. They open white. Then a hairline of pink edges each petal, widening and spreading day by day until the flowers slowly become a deep pink.

The other oddment in this scratch lot of tulips had an exactly similar habit, only in this case the bulb produces a single flower, belonging, I believe, to the Cottage group and thus taller than the Candelabra variety. It too was white, and it too developed a hairline of color around each petal. Only the color of this tulip was scarlet, quite horrid against the house, but fascinating to watch as the vivid color deepened and spread. The popular name for this variety is Chameleon.

Discouraged by this failure with tulips I flanked the faithful lily-flowered ones with Crown Imperial, in front of which I have recently added groups of La Riante, one of the white modern hybrid narcissus with a shallow, tangerine-colored cup.

Thus, with the space under the windows filled with bulbs and petunias from spring until frost, I turned to the corresponding strips between the paths and the fence.

Actually it was the generosity of two gardening friends that solved this problem for me. A neighbor from across the river in New Hampshire brought me one day so large a collection of coral-bells that I was surprised as well as pleased. Now I realize that he could be so lavish because the plants multiply with such speed. Those he gave me edged the path to the garden on the fence side for nearly its entire length. At the end of that first summer I was able to divide the plants into enough to finish the edging of that path and also to fringe the corresponding path to the north. Since then I have taken to canvassing my garden acquaintances each fall in order to dispose of my excess plants. Had I only known that this was the way of coral-bells I would have taken the name and address of a passer-by who admired them.

One morning a handsome sports car with the top down drew up at the curb, and a cultivated woman's voice called to me. "Would you be kind enough to tell me," she asked, "where you got coral-bells that color? The only ones I can find are red." At the moment I had to explain with regret that mine were a gift—that I had no idea where one could buy them.

My coral-bells are almost exactly the same dusty pink as the house. Once their tall, wiry stems shake out their clusters of little flowers about mid-June, so many more keep coming that an airy mist of pink seems to hover between the house and the fence for the rest of the summer.

The very few inches left between the coral-bells and the fence were filled with another gift. A man whose magnificent border of regal lilies is the pride of his heart found that he had to divide his overcrowded bulbs. When his job of replanting was done he brought me great clumps of those for which he had no room. I put them in against the fence. Now when they come into bloom about mid-July they literally stop passers-by in their tracks. Nearly two hundred great, white, gold-throated trumpets blared out over the fence last summer—a triumphant and glorious display.

The other spectacular feature of that planting in front of the house will sound like an anticlimax when the name is mentioned, but there is no anticlimax, I can assure anyone, about my morning-glories.

It is true, however, that many morning-glories have a bad name. Once on cultivated land they ramp and range, twist and twine, choking everything within reach. It is against the law to sell the seed of any morning-glory in the state of Arizona. Even here in Vermont, where our short season and cool nights prevent any Ipomoea from going on much of a rampage, the little wild morning-glory, bindweed, is a persistent garden pest.

Most of us are all too familiar with the common varieties of morning-glory we used to see climbing so swiftly up fence or lattice to screen the drying yard or, in an even more remote day, to lend a touch of softening color to the ubiquitous outhouse. But Heavenly Blue, which frames our front door, is no common morning-glory. It is an aristocrat.

When you come out of our house you step onto a good-sized square of concrete, protected overhead by a peaked roof of its own. This roof is supported by one of those white-painted trellised contraptions that can be bought from some of the larger mail-order houses. Nothing on earth would have induced my husband to buy such a structure, but it was in place when we bought the house, and I now sigh with relief that it is still there. An idea of supplanting it with small Doric columns was happily foiled by our inability to find Doric columns—any Doric columns let alone Doric columns of the right size.

About the middle of May I scratch a shallow trench on either side of the concrete slab and plant morning-glory seed. Sometimes I soak them overnight before planting, sometimes I don't—it doesn't seem to matter. As the vines push up I weed out those that would block the spaces opening out onto the paths and then let the other vines climb as they will up the strings my husband ties for them near the roof. They climb slowly at first, then swiftly spread an abundance of green to cover the latticed columns and wave up and onto the roof itself. When towards the end of July Heavenly Blue opens its great circles of bloom against the pink of the house and the white of the shutters, it is a sight to lift the heart.

Pink and blue and green and white are, I am well aware, a hackneyed color combination, but this is no common baby pink and baby blue. The color of the house is what artists call a "greyed-down" pink, much the color of the eighteenth-century bricks of the old houses in Annapolis, capitol of my native Maryland. The Heavenly Blue is the strong, luminous blue of the sky on the rarest of June days.

One August morning when I was on my knees inconspicuously weeding in the garden, I was startled by the scream of brakes as a car pulled in to the curb. Doors on both sides were flung open and banged shut. A man and a woman, each clutching a camera, raced toward the house and were instantly involved in strenuous efforts to capture this colorful bit of New England to take home to Idaho. They were far too absorbed in their task to notice me, and I purred with satisfaction in privacy.

Another couple whom we found enjoying our morning-glories was my old friend the Methodist minister and his wife. Literally dozens of people stopped to admire the morning-glories, but on one occasion these two, who knew our house and garden well, were staring all but open-mouthed. The display had never been more dazzling—and it was seven o'clock in the evening! This blue glory should have disappeared hours before.

It was that summer, an exceptionally cool and rainy one even for Vermont, that I learned just how temperamental morning-glories can be. Their bloom is conditioned, I discovered, strictly by temperature. As the world warms with the first light of a summer's day the flowers begin to open. By noon every vine is ablaze with color, but with a color that fades at the peak of the day's heat. The brilliant flowers shrivel and twirl into twists of wine color and white. The show is over until the next day.

That is the normal procedure, but on that evening when my clerical friend and his wife stood gazing in amazement at morning-glories in full bloom at 7 P.M. we were seeing the end of a day that had not adhered strictly to the conventional pattern of summer. It had been exceptionally cool. At six that morning the thermometer outside our front door had registered 44 degrees Fahrenheit, and since it had rained gently nearly all day the temperature did not rise much higher even at noon. About 4 P.M. the rain stopped, and I promptly went outside to take a look around. I found a number of morning-glory blossoms beginning to open as the late horizontal rays of the sun touched them. By the time our visitors had arrived the whole trellis was covered with a mass of bloom.

This particular incident occurred very early in September and was repeated several times before frost put an end to any further performance by my temperamental morning-glories. Just as the roots of the two words suggest, the temperamental nature of the flowers is dependent on the temperature of the season.

Not entirely, however, for like all living things morning-glories have their particular needs and requirements. One of these is lime, and this fact was dramatized for me by a story that a friend told me last year.

Molly is the wife of a mining engineer whose work takes him to wild and remote parts of the world seldom seen by a white man, let alone by a white woman. In just such a place, high in the mountains of central Mexico, Molly and Ed came upon Heavenly Blue morning-glories. The sweep of brilliant blue that covered a small meadow on one side of the trail was so startling that they both drew rein. As they looked, they saw that the little meadow was not entirely covered with the flowers—almost, but not quite. At the far side of the field the blue ended abruptly in a wavering line. The remaining few hundred yards of open land was green up to the dark belt of trees where the forest began again. Molly and Ed rode up to this sharp line of demarcation and Ed swung himself off his mule to investigate.

"Limestone," he reported coming back to Molly. "Those morning-glories are growing in shallow soil on a ledge of limestone. They stop dead when they come to the underlying granite."

No garden book, stating the sober fact that morning-glories like lime, could possibly make that useful piece of information so vivid.

Perhaps the concrete slab against which they are planted has supplied my morning-glories with the lime they need. But whatever the reason, Heavenly Blue has presented me with a display—to understate matters—of which no gardener need feel ashamed.

Altogether those meager inches in front of our house have served me better than I had dared to hope.

Lad's-Love, Dusty Miller,
and Morning Mist

Lad's-love, Dusty Miller, and Morning Mist—here are names that dance on the tongue. Yet, for all that these three Artemisias are as charming as their names, they are or can be as useful in the garden as a broom is in the house. Their blossoms bring no beauty to the borders. In fact, when the rather spindly spires of flowers begin to show, that is the time to start clipping. The value of these plants lies in the color and texture of their foliage, in their stance and habit of growth. They make fine accents in the garden. Those that are silver grey, for example, can call sharp attention to a certain spot or can define an area that might otherwise pass unnoticed.

To take the least glamorous first, it was Dusty Miller that eventually solved the problem of those eighteen inches outside the fence, running along the whole width of out street frontage. When we first bought our house this long narrow strip of land was given over almost exclusively to crab grass, and, while legally ours, it did seem obviously in the public domain. It was, however, such an eyesore that I prevailed upon the boy who cut the grass next door to run his mower along it every now and then, although even after a fresh mowing it continued to look dusty and dishevelled. Yet for a year or two I ignored its bedraggled condition. I had enough and more than enough to do behind the fence and in the garden.

It was the garden itself that finally made me consider the possibilities of those eighteen inches. When I faced the fact that, thanks to shade, I could not have, among other desirable things, any iris in my garden, I cast about for a place—some place, any place—where iris could be planted. For to me a garden without iris is painful. That strip outside the fence got more sunlight than any other part of our property, so I happily strung iris rhizomes down its full length, looking forward to the day when the sheaves of blue-green, swordlike leaves would take over the whole area and supply me with rainbow-colored flowers throughout June. But I reckoned without salt.

In winter our efficient snow removal system comes into play. An engaging miniature snowplow charges down the sidewalk, a truck trailing respectfully in its wake along the street. From the truck men fling shovelfuls of sand, liberally mixed with salt, on the newly swept sidewalk.

I describe this procedure for the benefit of those who live in or near our great East-coast cities. There a catastrophically heavy snowfall is so unusual that no community can afford to keep adequate equipment on hand to deal with it. And who doesn't know either from experience or from telecasts of the paralysis that overtakes such towns and cities when a heavy snowstorm strikes? But in northern New England even small villages such as ours stand expectant and ready with both men and machines.

When the snow finally melts the accumulated salt of the winter seeps naturally and promptly into my eighteen inches. This I learned to my sorrow that first spring after I had planted so many iris. All but a few of the rhizomes were mushy with decay. Those few I have left untouched, and a number still survive to give me some bloom and spread a few fans of sword blades against the fence. But obviously iris could not be counted on to solve the problem of that strip of land.

It was just about at this point that still another kind neighbor from New Hampshire brought me a collection of plants from her garden. Among them were some spindly grey stems bearing silver grey leaves so pale as to be almost white.

"Be careful where you plant that Dusty Miller," this gardener warned me. "It will take over your whole garden if you don't keep it down."

Hers was a Dusty Miller which she and her husband had collected on the sand dunes of Cape Cod—*Artemisia stelleriana*. The florists' Dusty Miller, so inevitable among the gaudy geraniums and marigolds of Memorial Day decorations, is a derivative of *A. stelleriana*. There are a number of silver Artemisias, and several of them, I suspect, are called Dusty Miller indiscriminately—a shining example of the trickiness of common names in contrast to the precision of botanical terms.

Dusty Miller is just a name to us today, but once it evoked a vivid and familiar picture. Over a century ago more and more trains began hauling more and more grain to large centralized mills. But until the process was complete and specialization general, it was to the man who operated the little mill with the big wheel in the local stream that farmers brought their wheat and corn and rye to be ground. He was an important personage in his community. Songs and stories grew up about him and in all the songs and stories—no matter how long and lean he might be—he was round and rosy. But always, fat or lean, he was truly dusty.

These silvery Artemisias have too a history that goes back beyond gardens, beyond medicine, to a magic of a primitive past. Eleanor Sinclair Rohde speculated about the possibility that the aura of magic that still touches some of the legends about them may stem back to the awe that they inspired in primitive man. To come upon the spectral greyness of such a ghostly plant growing in the darkness of a primeval forest must have sent many a shiver down many a primitive spine. It is at least a not implausible theory.

To return, however reluctantly, to the twentieth century and my New England village, I suddenly realized that any plant eager to take over the whole garden might just as well expend its energies on my problem strip. So I grubbed up some crab grass and planted the Dusty Miller.

While I was at work a neighbor who lived just "down street", as we say in Vermont, came by and stopped to talk. I showed her what I was doing and mentioned that I wished I had more plants—these not being nearly enough to get the job properly started.

"You are welcome to all you can weed out of my garden," said my friend. "The stuff is not only choking everything in my borders but it is coming up in the gravel paths. The more you take the happier I shall be."

With a bushel basket of roots from that garden I planted my inches and found my problem solved.

It is all but incredible that Dusty Miller or any other plant could solve it, for in addition to that dose of salt in winter those eighteen inches are mercilessly exposed to stray dogs and passing children. Each spring I look down at the short grey shoots breaking ground and reconcile myself to finding them irreparably damaged as the youngsters veer off the concrete sidewalk onto mother earth. But the tough stems take it and somehow survive. And on behalf of the children I should add that, once the plants are high enough to be noticeable to any but my peering eyes, few of the young ones fail to respect them. My Dusty Miller has flourished and multiplied. Salt, perhaps thanks to the Cape Cod provenance of my plants, does not bother them at all. From either side of our entrance path to either end of our fence I now have a thick, low hedge of pure silver, which admittedly would be handsomer if I clipped it more faithfully than I do. My carelessness is, however, rewarded by an abundance of silver sprays that are rather more than effective when placed in a bouquet of pink roses or, for that matter, among any garden flowers.

Just as Dusty Miller solved one problem for me, so Lad's-love solved another. My two little bushes of southernwood, as Lad's-love is more commonly called, give me a threefold pleasure. They are useful, deliciously fragrant, and interesting because of associations with man that stretch back across the centuries.

The usefulness of Lad's-love to me lies in the fact that the beautifully round, feathery little bushes stand guard at strategic points. The two little strips of land inside the fence, planted now with coral-bells and lilies, come to a dead-end against the short path that leads from the street to our front door. Before I planted them with coral-bells and lilies, there was not only an unfinished look to those two spots, but each offered a gap between the fence and the trellis over the door, a gap very inviting to curious dogs and children.

Evergreens seemed an obvious answer, so I brought a pair of small hemlocks in from the woods. Sturdy as they are they failed to survive the mounds of smothering snow flung over them by the boy who shovels our path. Then a friend brought me a couple of small fir trees from her hunting camp in the mountains, and they too succumbed. Cultivated dwarf evergreens would, I thought, best answer my purpose, but before I could get around to buying them I found the solution to this problem no more than a dozen feet from my own garden.

To the south of us is a big clapboard house divided into apartments. The old lady, eighty-one that summer, who has the whole first floor, liked to sit on the front porch, and when the little lawn around it grew unsightly she cut the grass herself. She was pushing the mower with surprising vigor one morning when I came out into the garden and, seeing her, went up to the wire fence on our southern border to talk to her. After the weather had been disposed of—it was too hot these days to cut the grass except early in the morning—she glared down and said irritably, "I wish that old thing was out of here. It keeps getting in my way." And she gave a vicious jab of the mower toward the object of her distaste. It was no more than an indeterminate lump of green to me, so I turned toward the picket fence, swung myself over, and joined her. The obstruction in the lawn that so annoyed her proved to be a very old bush of southernwood, unkempt and ragged and certainly no ornament in that small square of grass. To her great satisfaction I dug it up and carried it home.

The old bush divided easily into two plants. I set one in each of the gaps beside the path, where they now serve me not only as a deterrent to intruders but as delightful ornaments to our entrance. In the late fall I cut them back almost to the ground, and the mounds of snow that replace them in winter seem to do them no harm whatsoever.

It happens that their situation so near the front door is exactly right. Southernwood should always be planted at a spot where people stop, whether to look at something or to talk. Then the experienced gardener's hand goes out to nip off a bit of the tasselled foliage. Whether you are standing to look at a garden or a view or are standing just to talk to a friend or neighbor, you can crush the finely dissected leaves gently and sniff their very special fragrance.

Southernwood, Lad's-love—both names carry overtones of the shrub's story in gardens and of its association with man, which has been a long, and, on man's part, an affectionate one. I for instance enjoy my little bushes all the more because Lad's-love was one of the very first plants given me for the first garden I ever made. Amy Murray, who had brought me the rooted cutting, knew it as southernwood or Old Man but with her poet's sensitivity to words would have been delighted with the other name, Lad's-love, not only for its sound but also because of the story with which the name originated.

English country lads, so the tale goes, sighing to look more manly than their years in the eyes of their sweethearts, used to burn a branch or two of the bush and put the ashes into an ointment, which they rubbed optimistically over those areas where a beard should grow.

One cannot help wondering who was that bright but unknown lad who made this adaptation of a very ancient remedy for baldness. It appears over and over again in the old herbals that served as guides to home care of the sick in days when doctors were few, widely scattered, and far too expensive a luxury for ordinary folk. These herbals describe medications for everything from the common cold to hydrophobia, and they also give cosmetic receipts and even household hints in which herbs can be used. Rose water can keep a busy housewife's hand soft and white. The petals of this or that red flower can be crushed and rubbed on cheeks to impart a rosy glow. The ashes of southernwood will check that premature baldness that so trouble a man who is vain and still comparatively young.

Among the household hints is another use for southernwood. Sprigs of the bush, dried and laid among woolen clothes, protect them from moths. *Garde-robe,* the French call it. Modern housewives who use a pressure bomb—which perhaps not only exhales a dangerous substance but flaunts an unpronounceable name—need not smile with superiority at this quaint idea. It was prevalent in Shakespeare's time, it is true, and in all probability long before that, but it is far from dead today. My old lady of the lawn mower came to me the following summer to ask if she might gather some sprigs from the plant she had given me. A friend had told her that they would be a sure protection for her winter clothes. More surprising still, no less an authority than the English Royal Horticultural Society's *Dictionary of Gardening* credits this property to a closely related species. Perhaps those of us who have taken to heart Rachel Carson's warnings about modern chemicals should turn to our Artemisias!

Southernwood is cultivated in England as well as here, and it seems obvious that the origin of its name is due to the fact that to England and north Europe this was quite literally southern wood, a plant native to the southern part of the Continent, especially to Spain and to Italy.

By whatever name, from whatever country, it has been familiar in American gardens from the early days. It is always counted as one of the old-fashioned plants beloved by our grandmothers. It is just as useful today and just as ornamental as it has been for generations.

Morning Mist, by contrast, is a newcomer to our gardens. Silver Mound, our catalogues call it, but when I first saw it not many years ago I privately rechristened it Silver Velvet, for velvet was the substance that my fingers remembered as I ran my hands across the silver cushion. Whereupon a friend gave my fingers another memory when she exclaimed, "Why it feels just like baby's hair." However, I have personally settled for the English name, Morning Mist. It sounds like something out of a lyric, which is as it should be, because the plant is the visual equivalent of a lyric.

For those who don't happen to know it, Morning Mist is a little shrub no more than eight inches high, branching in such a way that the foliage makes a round, flat cushion of pale jade green so overlaid with silver that the basic color is barely perceptible. That description is inadequate, but I do not know how to find more precise or evocative words.

To haul this airy thing down to its utilitarian level, Morning Mist is recommended as an edging plant or for rock gardens. In a garden as small as mine it would take up too much room as an edging plant, so I have tried to use it here and there as an accent. Please note the word "tried." And the reader may remember that at the beginning of this chapter I said that the Artemisias I am describing "are or could be as useful" etc. The qualification had to be included because of my own inadequacy. I have never succeeded in growing Morning Mist satisfactorily. I naturally blame every failure in my garden on shade, but even in sun the plant refuses to perform for me. I have begged Morning Mist, bought it, and had it given to me, but all to no avail. I have about come to the conclusion—quite seriously I may add—that, like the African Violet, Morning Mist refuses to respond to my affection for it. It does not like, let alone love me. This is a situation well calculated to bring any gardener into a properly humble state of mind, and perhaps this is the destined role of Morning Mist in my garden.

7

Garden Gadgets
and Gimmicks

A gadget, according to my own private dictionary, is an ingenious object used for the purpose for which it was manufactured. A gimmick is an object used with ingenuity for some purpose other than that for which it was originally intended.

In a garden as tiny as mine few gadgets are useful, since they tend to be labor saving devices for gardeners who cultivate large or largish areas. Where there is no lawn there is no need for a power mower. Where there is only one small tree an auger drill for fertilizing would be superfluous. Where beds and borders are small, a tank spray would be more trouble than it is worth. In fact I get along nicely with no more than three gadgets, and only one of these is at all notable.

The common whirling spray attached to the garden hose does very well for me and is familiar to everyone. "Soakease" is not quite so well known, but I find it convenient. It too is an attachment for the hose, and its long green tubes can be adjusted now near to one section of the garden, now to another, each tube giving special attention to this or that group of plants by letting a gentle, steady stream of water flow wherever it will do the most good. My third gadget, despised and rejected by gardeners at one of the great municipal flower shows, has served me so well that it rates a kind word and also another word as to how I came into possession of it.

Some years ago a friend of mine, a manufacturer of various small metal objects, had what he thought was a good idea for a gadget for weeding. He had a piece of heavy metal strip, not quite an inch wide, bent into a diamond shape and then set in a collar. This was fastened to a wooden handle such as those used for trowels. It is quite true that this implement would be of little use in a large garden, but in a rock garden or a garden as small as mine it is invaluable. A sprightly colony of Chickweed seedlings can be disposed of by the sharp point of the gadget with far greater speed and efficiency than would be possible with a hand cultivator. When these or other weed seedlings appear close to some cherished rarity in the rock garden, again the shallow scratching point takes care of them with speed and precision. In fact I have found this minor invention very handy indeed.

The inventor of this gadget had a number of samples made up and put them on display at one of the famous flower shows. When no orders were forthcoming my friend abandoned his idea, but a few years later, when he and his wife stopped by to see us, he brought along one of his rejected gadgets as a present to a gardening friend. I have been grateful ever since.

Abandoning at this point any attempt to retain my etymological distinctions between gadgets and gimmicks, I turn now to the waterfall, which is the chief ornament of the garden pool. It is true that the copper tubing which supplies the water was probably manufactured to convey water, but I doubt if any manufacturer ever anticipated that his product would be used quite as we have used it.

During the first years the pool was in place we stocked it with goldfish. That phrase, as I write it, sounds pompous—"stocked it with goldfish." The process consisted simply in tracing down which of the so-called dime stores in our neighborhood had goldfish for sale and then acquiring half a dozen. These were sufficient to handle the problem of mosquito eggs, and that, so far as we were concerned, was the whole duty of goldfish. One spring, however, when even the few we needed proved elusive, my husband pointed out that mosquitos do not lay eggs in running water. If a trickle of water flowed in one end of the pool and out the other, the mosquito problem would be solved without benefit of goldfish.

With this idea in mind he then proceeded to buy forty or fifty feet of half-inch copper tubing. The plumber came and attached one end of the tube to the outlet pipe which supplies my garden hose. Then we did the rest.

Carrying the heavy loops of tubing my husband walked slowly backward, paying out a short strip at a time. From the outlet pipe the tubing was carried west to the picket fence, then along the full length of the garden at the foot of the fence until in the south corner it was carried around the trunk of a hemlock and bent at an angle to reach the edge of the pool. What had seemed offhand a rather complicated matter proved to be incredibly swift and easy. As my husband paid out the tube I trenched rapidly with a trowel. The tube lay never more than two or three inches below the surface. It is true that before the summer was over some of my shallow trenching was washed away and a garish glitter of copper lay exposed to view. But a hasty trowelful of earth, well tamped down, covered the unsightly gleam for the rest of the season. Later, time took care of the matter for us. The bright copper has weathered down to so inconspicuous a dull brown that if a bit of the tubing shows here or there above ground it is no more noticeable than a stray twig.

Where the end of the tube reached the edge of the pool I built enough rockwork around it so that it would not show at all. The trickle that emerges from under one rock to flow softly over another into the pool looks so natural that at first some of our neighbors found it hard to believe it was not just a happy accident. So to prove the artificiality of the contrivance I would walk back to the house and turn the petcock that controlled the flow of water. Up would come a gay fountain, splashing importantly into the pool. I always readjusted the water back to a trickle after my demonstration and thus it usually remains all summer, from late May until the early frosts of September. Our village is blessed by a copious supply of perfectly delectable water unsullied by chemicals. As the supply is far greater than the population needs, my conscience is clear about using water so lavishly. The overflow from our little pool goes back as it should, clean and clear, into the surrounding earth and from there passes into the cycle on which we all depend for life.

It was a pleasant surprise to find that our rather primitive house-to-pool water system survived the rigor of Vermont winters without any protection whatever. The outlet pipe in the foundation of the house is, of course, disconnected once cold weather has set in, and the first year I felt guilty when for some reason I failed to supply the copper tubing with at least a light blanket of peat moss. Somewhere as it lay along the irregular ground, I felt sure, a little water must have collected, and I feared it would burst, as heavier pipes do when frozen under similar conditions. But it stood up to 28 degrees below like a hero and has continued to do so ever since. Were I native born I would have ended that last sentence with the cautious Vermont qualification "at least so fur!"

Now I turn to the true gimmicks, which are the joy of my life.

The first is chicken wire cut into eighteen-inch squares. Toward the middle of May, here in central Vermont, the first red lacquer shoots of peonies begin to break ground. It is then that I get out my squares of chicken wire. A square is laid over each plant, and the sprouts continue to push up through the wide meshes. As the stems lengthen and the leaves unfold, the wire is lifted gently. By the time the plants have reached full growth, the wire, pulled as high as it will go, disappears under the over-arching leaves to remain in place throughout the season. No further staking is required. When a bad storm rages, even if complete with hail, the gardener who has used chicken wire need not have peonies on his mind. Blossoms may of course be bruised and beaten, but thanks to this gimmick the plants stand firm and shapely. My two single Japanese peonies give me great satisfaction. Even after the all-too-short season of bloom is over, the rounded balls of dark green leaves are still handsome as a garden ornament.

This helpful hint about chicken wire was passed along to me by a charming woman who had, with her husband, acquired a place near Old Chatham, New York. The large garden near the old house was in very bad condition, and one of the major problems the new owners faced was what to do about scores and scores of peonies. They shared with me a distaste for the com-mercial wire fencing in which so many peonies are so unhappily enclosed. In addition to that the cost of such fencing would be considerable and the labor involved daunting, to say the least. Just as they had decided with regret that they would have to dispose of most of the plants, a neighbor suggested the chicken-wire treatment. Now their June display of peonies is a matter of pride and delight.

Another gimmick that I value highly is the coat hanger. It is perfectly absurd for a mature adult to derive as much pleasure as I do from transforming an object intended for the convenience of my wardrobe into a stake for supporting my plants. To do this I grasp the neck of the coat hanger in the left hand and seize the crossbar with the right. I then pull until what was originally a horizontal object becomes a vertical one. My pleasure in this simple performance has nothing whatever to do with gardening. Always as I pull there slips into my mind the memory of a small tomboy, arrow fitted to the string, tugging at the bow she herself has made according to the directions so happily supplied to children by Ernest Thompson Seton more than half a century ago.

To return to the garden and the gimmick. The contrivance thus brought into being is a short garden stake of almost incredible efficiency. The rounded end pushes easily into good garden soil and the two upright wires serve as the shaft of the stake. The hook at the top can be bent in any direction or adjusted to any angle to support anything that needs to be supported except the tallest plants. One morning I came out into the garden to find two clumps of Tradescantia beaten nearly flat by a storm of the night before. I tucked three coat hangers inconspicuously into place around each plant and wove string from one hook to another to encircle the whole; the plants remained trim and tidy for the rest of the summer. A single plant that needs it can be given support by means of the coat hanger without the tiresome complexity of string and stake, and the black wires show very little among the leaves. Furthermore, the method tends to solve the problem of what to do with that apparently inexhaustible supply of coat hangers with which nearly every housewife is burdened. In fact I find it hard to keep within the bounds of restraint in celebrating the virtues of the coat hanger in the garden.

Another gimmick that I occasionally use in spring is the brown paper bag obtainable at any grocery store. Whenever I have a flat or two of seedling annuals to transplant I have, like everyone else, the problem of keeping them shaded until they are established. Naturally, the best way to do this is to rig up some sort of an awning, but there are spots in many a garden such as mine where this is not practicable. I then resort to paper bags. These I buy quite a bit larger than the plants I wish to protect. I open out each bag, cut four slits at the open end, and then fit the bag over a transplanted seedling. The slits permit you to flatten out the ends of the bag against the ground, and handfuls of earth piled on the flattened paper anchors the bag for the day or two necessary to give the seedling protection. The bags stand up surprisingly well even during a heavy rain.

All gardeners find certain gadgets useful, but somehow the gimmicks that we contrive for ourselves have a soul-satisfying quality that no factory can supply.

8

Horticultural

Horrors

Three plants, two words, and all artificial flowers make up my very personal list of horticultural horrors.

Many a disapproving eyebrow may be raised because I have not included weeds on my list. But weeds are not horrors—just nuisances. Furthermore, all my horrors are preventable, while weeds are merely incvitable. Finally, as I have already admitted in the case of the little brown sorrel, I cherish a shamefaced affection for quite a few weeds. I can eradicate crab grass, knotweed, and the two most common plantains with zest, but what gardener does not resent the need for grubbing up jill-o'er-theground? It is a true weed, troublesome and difficult to eradicate, but I like to remember that its singing name figured in a poem and that the plant itself once had importance in an ancient industry.

Here, where the moors stretch free,
In the high blue afternoon,
Are the marching sun and talking sea
And the racing winds that wheel and flee
On the flying heels of June.

Jill-o'er-the-ground is purple blue,
Blue is the Quaker-Maid,
The wild geranium holds its dew
Long in the boulder's shade.

"Gloucester Moors," written by William Vaughn Moody in the 1890's, is no great work of art, but it lingers in my mind because it is filled with the birds and the flowers and the color of the rocky Eastern coastline that stretches from northern Massachusetts through Maine up into Canada.

Moody's Jill has a name that must seem appropriate to many gardeners since the old English Jill, which derives from the Latin Juliana, suggests a flighty wench. Most of us would agree that the picture of a feckless female, decorative and pretty, flaunting herself inconveniently all over the place, makes a nice parallel to our own charming garden nuisance. But a distinguished botanist hauls us down to less frivolous levels. In his useful and interesting little book, *Weeds of Lawn and Garden,* Dr. John M. Fogg, Jr., finds that in this particular case 'Jill' or 'Gill,' as it was often written in earlier times, suggests nothing flightier than a manufacturing process. His Gill-over-the-ground could be an old English corruption of the French verb *guiller* and would thus refer to the fact that, in the days when manufacturing was largely a household affair, the leaves of the plant were used to ferment and clarify beer and ale.

Celandine is another weed that I eradicate with regret. Although its yellow flowers are small, the plant itself is shapely, in fact quite beautiful. But, unfortunately, given only half a chance, it would soon have any garden to itself. When you watch its determined efforts to spread far and wide, it is not hard to see how Gold Street in lower Manhattan came by its name some two hundred years ago.

Then there is Creeping Charlie, its penny-shaped leaves and dime-sized flowers, accounting for the other name, moneywort, that I knew in my Maryland childhood: purslane or pusley, a plump little herb of shiny red stems and fat dark leaves; and that infinitesimal veronica, a weed of lawns rather than of gardens, whose minute white flowers on barely more than an inch-high spike are blue-veined and perfect. All weeds, every one of them, weeds that must be kept down or pulled up, but they can hardly be classed as horrors.

One of my real horrors, however, if it does not cause the twitch of a single eyebrow may well elicit a murmur of dissent. In fact, judging by the scope of a comparatively new industry, I must be almost alone in my fanatical distaste for artificial flowers. Now that they have gone into mass production it is evident that someone, millions of someones, must be buying them, for these travesties of plants sprout everywhere. The meat counter of the supermarket that I patronize sometimes displays little "arrangements" of too blue forget-me-nots and too pink baby roses and, at Easter, so-called madonna lilies in plastic pots swathed in purple crepe paper.

Time was when artificial flowers were restricted almost exclusively to female headgear. The wreaths of cornflowers, daisies, and poppies that adorned the hats my sisters and I used to wear to Sunday school were pleasant and gay, but my mother would have shuddered at the idea of such flowers on her dinner table:

a place for everything and everything in its place. The place for artificial flowers was on a hat.

This brings me to a qualification which I should perhaps have made when I first mentioned artificial flowers—*all* artificial flowers. I like artificial flowers on hats and I do not mind them too much in such things as Christmas decorations, where they do not pretend to be anything but the imitations they are. To find them posing in pots and baskets as the real thing is an abomination. Nor can I find anything better to say for the more expensive specimens to be found in specialty shops. Some of the imported varieties are exquisitely made, but they are dead things—about as satisfactory to a flower lover as a doll would be as a substitute for a baby.

As may be seen from the foregoing diatribe, my horrors are very personal ones, not, I am sure, shared by everybody. But at least it is safe to assume that most gardeners have their own private lists, so without further apology I continue with mine.

The three plants that arouse my particular spleen are cannas, golden glow, and scarlet sage.

Cannas loomed large in my childhood—literally large, for I was always small for my age. The huge plants with their coarse, ungraceful leaves towered menacingly over me as they stood in the circle that centered the driveway beside our house. Their uncompromising scarlet and yellow flowers had no appeal for the child who had found the spot where the only showy orchids in the neighborhood grew; who could have gone blindfolded to the great oak between whose spreading roots the first delicate pink and white and blue hepaticas appeared in spring; who knew the stream along whose bank the glorious red of cardinal-flowers glowed at midsummer and the meadow in whose dusty tangle one could find the orange butterfly weed. I doubt that

I ever thought of cannas as having any relationship whatsoever to my private discoveries. I disliked them not because they differed so extravagantly from the wild flowers I loved but because of their grossness, their lack of grace, and their crude uncompromising colors. They revolted me then and they still revolt me. Modern catalogues are advertising a new, smaller variety of the plant, but not even a miniature canna could tempt me.

Golden glow has mercifully receded from most contemporary gardens, although sometimes only at the expense of great toil. It is a plant that spreads with the most ferocious efficiency and hangs on in the face of the most persistent efforts to eradicate it. The tousled yellow flowers in thick clusters at the top of tall ungainly stems have, for me at any rate, no virtue that cannot be supplied more satisfactorily by marigolds and heleniums.

Golden glow appeared on the horticultural horizon toward the beginning of this century, when it was welcomed as a fascinating novelty, a completely double form of our native *Rudbeckia laciniata*. In *A Woman's Hardy Garden,* published in 1903, Helena Rutherford Ely gave the new discovery her blessing, and it was extensively planted. Mrs. Ely was undoubtedly as bemused by *art nouveau,* bird's eye maple furniture, and Favrile glass as were any of her contemporaries, so it is not surprising that she should have found in golden glow a fine new furnishing for her garden. Thus the plant took its place among other extravaganzas of the period—the nadir of taste in this country. Many of the stands of golden glow that one sees now here and there may well date back to that time, for this is the only plant I know more difficult to eradicate than *Sedum sarmentosum.*

Scarlet sage, the third plant on my list, is actually less of a horticultural horror than a horticultural cliché. Whenever an inexperienced gardener wants to "brighten up" a bit of land, scarlet sage is sure to put in an appearance. It used to be all but standard in the beds near railroad stations in the days when railroad stations were tidy enough and prosperous enough to indulge in such luxuries as ornamental plantings. Now, tastefully combined with magenta petunias and orange and yellow marigolds, it often does duty helping to "brighten up" our already far from drab gas stations.

In itself scarlet sage is an exceptionally handsome plant, with its steady spike of inflorescence and horizontally spread leaves. The trouble with it of course is its color, for nothing is more difficult to handle satisfactorily than a crude red. Move from primary red toward a deep warm salmon and on down through gradations of pink to the faintest apple blossom, and all along the line you get something subtle and lovely. Or you may turn to the cool side of the spectrum and run through red-purple and magenta on down into increasingly pale warm lavenders. All these variations lend themselves with more or less grace to colors nearby, whether the colors are on a house, a gas station, or just in other flowers in the garden. Primary color lends itself to nothing. It is an uncompromising statement—a shout raised either to startle or to offend.

Not long ago, however, I saw scarlet sage used to great advantage. On the outskirts of a neighboring town the tidiest cottage imaginable is centered on a square of bright green lawn, the whole surrounded with a low privet hedge. The cottage is painted an immaculate white, its shutters and front door a vivid scarlet. On either side of the path that runs from the street to that front door are narrow borders planted with nothing but Scarlet Sage. Here, if ever, is a shout to attract attention but, if it is not too much a contradiction in terms, a demure sort of shout. At any rate it is charming.

Strong colors close to their primary origin can be handled, but it takes great skill and taste to accomplish the feat. Mexicans are adepts at it, as all who have been to Mexico know.

Some years ago I received a Christmas card from one of Mexico's finest modern artists, the late Miguel Covarrubias. On a stiff little white card Covarrubias had painted a small medallion of the Madonna and Child in a narrow oval no more than two inches high. Yet in the space of that miniature he had used scarlet, magenta, orange, shrill bright green, and ultramarine blue. The brilliance of the green and the depth of the blue brought the other usually clashing colors into harmony—an exotic, exciting sort of harmony but a satisfying one. I have often wondered since about the possibility of transferring just such a color scheme into the garden, but I doubt that any except a Mexican could manage it successfully. Certainly I could not.

Now I turn to two words that are the last items on my list of horticultural horrors, though by no means the least. My distaste for "Glad" and "Mum" is so acute that I am unable to write or utter either of these distressing diminutives without quotation marks.

Their use is now so wide-spread that I cannot think they seeped naturally into the language by word of mouth. That method operates slowly, but "Glad" and "Mum" have swept into so-called garden literature with almost the speed of light. Quite possibly they sprouted full blown on Madison Avenue where their brevity would be an obvious advantage in advertisements featuring gladiolii and chrysanthemums. It is harder to view with sympathy the undiscriminating acceptance of these verbal mutilations by the garden world. Reputable garden magazines use them freely and all too many gardeners have followed their lead.

The trouble with "Glad" is that it is so cute. The handsome and dignified ornament of our summer gardens deserves better than that. Admittedly its full name is not particularly attractive. It carries no geographical or historical connotations, nor is it musical. Furthermore, it has so alien a sound to our ears that many gardeners soften its last syllable into an apologetic ah— "gladiolah," This steers the word clear of the plural "gladioli." In a language without case endings this compromise—"gladiola, gladiolas"—should be acceptable to all but the most pedantic. At least it is preferable to "Glad."

Chrysanthemum, in sharp contrast, is not only a fine word in itself but is rich in connotations. No one with an ear for the music of words can fail to catch the lilt in the third syllable and, along with that music, overtones of the plant's history and background. A conventionalized form of the flower has long been the national emblem of Japan. There, and in China, comparatively undistinguished little wild composites were bred and bred again, crossed and recrossed into the flowers that, in all their variety of form and color, bring splendor to our autumn gardens.

The Oriental origin of this garden ornament is so well known that only a single flashback is needed to bring into focus the gulf that lies between the good name chrysanthemum and the bastard "Mum." Can anyone possibly picture a Chinese gentlemen of the old school slowly pacing his garden paths to admire his "Mums?"

If mine seems an overzealous protest against such verbal mutilations as "Glad" and "Mum," there may be a psychological explanation for it. In a greatly troubled world it is a relief to find an uncomplicated issue in whose behalf—to change the metaphor—one may draw one's sword with a flourish. Crusades have been very fashionable of late years. Let us then, as gardeners, mount a crusade in hehalf of our specialized vocabulary, which has so much richness and beauty worth defending. *À bas* "Glads" and "Mums". *Aux armes, jardiniers!*

9

Spring

Spring comes with a rush to northern New England. In the brief six weeks from the first of May to mid-June the flowering world up here makes a mighty but never wholly successful effort to catch up with that of gentler climates farther south.

The drama of that wild scurry into bloom was made very vivid for me in the years when we still lived in New York but went to New Hampshire every summer to run a small museum there. We used to leave our house, less than thirty miles up the Hudson from the George Washington Bridge, on a morning during the first week in May. Trees were in young but full leaf, tulips and lilacs in bloom, bees busy among the first honey-sweet wisteria blossoms; and the old apple tree had sent up above its tilted trunk three big puffs of pink and green, the pink to fade later to white as the blossoms opened.

By sunset we would reach a land where leaves were still thin and tiny on the skeletons of trees, the fields straw-colored and drab, gardens and cultivated areas naked with newly turned earth. Always when we arrived we found a vase holding a few yellow daffodils to welcome us, set out on the kitchen table by the caretaker's wife. Hundreds of these had finished blooming outside my own living room windows at home nearly a month before.

Back in New York, March had long since blown gold and white and purple bubbles that opened into crocuses above last year's dark wet leaves. Against the twig-strewn earth, pale straplike leaves surrounded slim green stems from which dangled the green-tipped bells of snowflakes. April and the west wind had brought daffodils even as in England, and huge masses of golden forsythia had foamed up in the shrubbery borders. Spring there had come slowly, gently, but steadily over many weeks.

Not so in New England. When I used to explore that New Hampshire garden on the first morning after we had arrived there would be no sign of color whatever, except here and there the electric blue flash of squills or perhaps another yellow daffodil just opening.

Yet in an incredibly short time everything seemed to burst into bloom simultaneously. The tiny balled buds on the apple trees swelled to pink. More daffodils appeared—then tulips and lilacs. Jacob's-ladder and lilies of the valley made a charming combination of blue and white. By Memorial Day there were even early peonies and iris in bloom.

Now that I live permanently in this same neighborhood, across the Connecticut River, I still watch that mad dash into bloom with wonder, but now too with all the Vermonter's hunger for color after the long white winter.

It was not until after we had bought our house on Main Street that I had ever seen April in New England. It is a dim, colorless, shadowy month, bringing much rain, the "mud season," and little more promise of bloom than the tips of things just beginning to push out of the still half-frozen ground. There are the tips of green where daffodils will be, dark purplish blue knobs close to the ground from which Mertensia will unfold, the shining, sharp red spear-tips that will be peonies. It is not until the middle of the month that gay little squills flash their brilliant blue. They start up first only in odd sunny spots—between the stones of paved paths where they have been dropped by accident or in out-of-the-way corners. Only in the last week or ten days of April does the neat, tight ring of these squills come into full bloom under the bare branches of my dwarf apple tree. But by that time the crocuses too have appeared, and spring is on its way.

In my tiny garden, crocuses have been planted between a clump of Christmas roses and a southernwood bush just opposite one of the living room windows. At that time of year it is well to be able to contemplate flowers from the safe vantage point of warmth within doors. Among the crocuses a few, too few, *Iris reticulata* spread their triple bands of dark purple velvet. The orange-red stamens of the crocuses burn with the brightest color in sight, since mine are all-white ones—white, and white veined with lavender. They are a promise of good things to come.

With crocuses, spring is on its way but rarely up here without setbacks. On the eighth of May, one year, the crocuses themselves disappeared under a respectable mantle of snow. On May thirtieth of another year, a devastating black frost did widespread damage to local apple and strawberry crops and wiped out the columbines, on which I had counted for bloom in June. In this climate, only with the most carefully chosen bulbs can one get a touch of color in the garden before April is over.

May, however, opens for me with a very special flower that is as majestic as its name—Crown Imperial. Since it is only beginning to be popular in American gardens, perhaps a description of it may not be out of place. From a large bulb a strong stem rises, fringed with leaves that are smaller but not unlike those of the regal lily. About twelve to fifteen inches from the ground the leaves end abruptly and the stem continues to rise until it is finished off with a jaunty tuft of leaves. Flower buds cluster under the tuft and hang down to open in varying shades of red, orange, and dull yellow bells around the space so cunningly left bare for them. Legend has it that these flowers were white when they grew in the Garden of Gethsemane, where they were often admired by Christ when He walked there. But after His night of agony in the garden the flowers turned red, and tears are now to be found within them.

This tale may be as farfetched as are most Christian flower legends. The Crown Imperial, a Fritillaria, is native to Persia, Afghanistan, and Kashmir and there is no proof it had reached Palestine by 33 A.D. It might have, of course, but so far as the Western world was concerned the plant was unknown until some bulbs were shipped from Constantinople to Vienna in 1576. From there it spread across Europe. Thus it was a new and "outlandish" plant in Elizabethan gardens, and much of my pleasure in the flower comes from its association with men and women of the time wise in gardening. Shakespeare and Marlowe knew it. Elizabeth herself admired the stately plant, and so undoubtedly did Bacon and Lord Burleigh. Two great gardeners of the period, John Gerard and John Parkinson, described the Crown Imperial with loving enthusiasm.

My first bulb bloomed for the first time on the first of May. Thus it was a truly royal herald which ushered in the whole colorful display as spring swept over the garden: tulips, lily-flowered, Cottage and Darwin; primroses and for-get-me-nots; pansies and bugle; sky-blue Virginia cowslips and bleeding heart.

Actually like every other dedicated gardener I would have long been out counting buds, watching sheaths break to show a touch of color. At first the summons of Crown Imperial would be answered only by a flower or two opening here and there. But always toward the middle of May there would come a wonderful morning when everything seemed to have burst into bloom overnight.

Tulips naturally dominate the garden at this time. I have finally achieved a collection with which I am well content, though this is no great virtue on my part, because it is hard to go wrong with tulips. In fact the only way I can think of is to plant a heterogeneous mixture of any or all colors, but if you stick to planting tulips for blocks of color the result can hardly fail to be delightful.

In the garden proper the long, shallow, semicircular bed which backs against the white fence is, when the tulips bloom, the main feature of my spring garden. The bed is filled with Rosy Wings, a Cottage tulip of a clear coral pink. One year I planted a formal triangle of three Mertensia clumps among these tulips, but Virginia cowslips do not readily lend themselves to formality. Now scattered casually here and there, volunteers spread out their shrill green leaves, topped by pink buds and bright blue bells among Rosy Wings. The outside curve of the semicircle is finished and framed by a single line of Mt. Tacoma, a double white tulip that does not grow as tall as Rosy Wings. Ordinarily I do not care much for double flowers, least of all double tulips, but Mt. Tacoma is as fine as some of the modern peonies which it resembles.

Still another tulip has come and gone in my garden before Rosy Wings and Mt. Tacoma bloomed but I record it in second place advisedly. Outside the ring of squills around my apple tree I had planted a circle of *Tulipa kaufmanniana,* the water-lily tulip. Color photographs in advertisements and garden magazines had led me to suppose that this little species tulip was white with a band of crimson down the outside of each petal. The crimson band was there, all right, but to my disappointment the flowers proved to be a soft, dull yellow. If you want your water-lily tulips white you must buy the more expensive *T. kaufmanniana ancilla,* which is described as having a rosy design at the center of its whiteness and an old-rose pink exterior. That exterior is important, because these little tulips have an endearing habit of folding towards sunset like praying hands. Each morning they open wide again.

With the first snow of November drifting down I have just finished planting a new circle of this white *kaufmanniana* around the squills, hoping that this time I may get the color effect I want.

Just across the path that defines the big tulip semicircle is a small clear area between perennials that blooms later. This I usually plant with primroses or pansies. One year I filled the space with steel-blue pansies packed tight. Another, I had a carefully arranged pattern of dark blue, cream-color, and pink primroses. One can never have enough primroses, so I always buy more than I need to grow opposite the tulips and tuck the extra ones here and there along the stone-paved paths—lovely small tufts of yellow, white, and pink. The dark blue are rarely to be had in quantity and are very hard to carry over our bitter winters.

Another blue, however, the bright clear blue of forget-me-nots, is as easy to get and as expansive as the dark blue primrose is rare and retiring. Several years ago I told the friend at whose nursery I was buying primroses that I thought I would like some forget-me-nots too. When I came to settle my account she refused to take a penny for the forget-me-nots. "I spend my time grubbing them out everywhere," she told me and added with a grin, "Just wait awhile. You will be doing the same thing yourself."

Well, not quite. I cannot bear to discard anything so charming. But I do grub them up, not a single plant or two at a time but in hunks, which I carry around and plant to enliven other places in the garden. As a result forget-me-nots are everywhere. They cluster around the feet of the Mt. Tacomas. They bob up among the primroses and pansies, sprout between the rocks around the pool, bloom on bare spaces which summer perennials will take over later, and generally brighten every corner of the garden.

Only two small areas defy them. Even forget-me-nots are unable to make any headway against the dense mats formed by the purple-bronze rosettes of Ajuga. They can only nudge in along the edges beside the paths and take up a point of vantage among those extra primroses I had planted there.

On the far side of my tiny pool are more primroses and, of course, forget-me-nots, among which I have planted the tubers of Dutchman's-breeches which a friend brought me last summer. I look forward with pleasure to their soft pink stems holding up the grey-green lacework of leaves and curves of white yellow-tipped flowers. They serve to remind me of a wide patch of them that I once knew, growing wild as they should, but now bull-dozed out of existence.

A cultivated cousin of theirs is the old-fashioned bleeding heart, which I am only too happy to have in my garden. Its deep pink buds make a fine display among the spring flowers. By the time they open the tulips have begun to drop their petals and the tufts of primroses are fading. Spring is over and summer is on the way.

10

When Summer
Comes
to Town

When summer comes to town it reaches my garden with peonies. Spring has drifted away in lilies of the valley, Jacob's-ladder and bleeding heart. Last year when the big saucers of my single white peonies opened, a mat of massed blue pansies lay between the two well rounded plants, and in the border behind them rich dark blue Tradescantia made an excellent background.

This planting has been mentioned before, as have most of the others listed here, but, for all that, I want to run briefly through the succession of summer bloom in order to bring the season into focus.

Regal lilies follow the peonies with a curving line of ten-inch-high Cheery Pink daylilies between them and the pansies. After these lilies and small daylilies have gone by, taller daylilies take over at the far ends and in the middle of the back border—wine-red, pink, and the palest of yellows—while various shades of rosy Impatiens and deep blue Browallia are getting into their stride to last out the summer. At the very back of the long border Cleome follows, to stand tall, handsome, and floriferous until frost cuts the big plants down. In the shallow semicircle against the fence, Ballerina, with its edging of Blue Mink, blooms steadily throughout the summer, and on the far side of the pool, in August, the thin stems of the smaller Funkia, *Hosta Lancifolia*, are hung with lilac trumpets. Along the fence side of the paths in front of the house, coral-bells shiver and quiver nearly all summer long, while on the other side white petunias tumble about between the paths and the house. August spangles the morning-glory vines over our door with Heavenly Blue, which keep crowding one another until frost.

When summer comes to town it is like being thirty-five again, a sort of tip-toe point in life. Then at last one can enjoy the flowering world on one's feet instead of on one's knees and savor the colorful achievement of many long hours of hard work. It is time, too, to look around and see what the neighbors are doing, for as every gardener knows there is both pleasure and profit in visiting the gardens of one's friends.

I remember one planting in a friend's garden with special pleasure, because it surmounted in triumph a color problem I would have considered insoluble. It happens that I detest the typical red-orange of Oriental poppies, largely because their shriek of color does violence to everything in their vicinity. Yet one of our village gardeners handled an outburst of the flaming giants with skill and success. In a section of her garden, isolated from the rest, is an outcrop of big granite boulders. Among these she has set a great many poppies and then added a generous supply of baby's breath, which rises like clouds of white steam through leaping flame, with the grey rocks and green hillside as background. Indeed, she has created as fine a spectacular as any Fourth of July celebration ever produced. Created it single-handed, I add with profound respect, in spite of the fact that a childhood attack of polio left both legs com-

pletely crippled, a handicap most people would consider insupera-
ble. Yet her garden as a whole, well planned, colorful, and fragrant, would do credit to the most able-bodied gardener.

Flower shows and garden tours burgeon all over the countryside when summer comes to town.

On garden tours I have seen many lovely gardens and have
often been entertained not only by unexpected sidelights but also
by the irrelevant reasons that bring many visitors on garden
tours.

I was taken on one garden tour by a friend who, after driving
her station wagon up an incredibly steep, wooded hillside, swung
it into a small gravelled parking lot behind the single building
in sight.

"This isn't a house," I protested. "It's a power station." For
the low, windowless rectangle, with an immensely tall brick
chimney at one end, looked exactly like a miniature of a power
station I used to see from the commuter's train that took me
into New York from Rockland County. My friend laughed, assured me that this was a masterpiece of modern architecture,
and led me around to the front of the house. What was undoubtedly in happier seasons a delightful garden fell away on steep
terraces at our feet, but that summer a devastating drought had
left it shabby and almost colorless. Turning away from this sad
spectacle I was dazed to find myself in the master bedroom. My
feet were still on the flagged terrace in front of the house but
I stood within touching distance of one of the twin beds in an
opulently furnished bedroom. The angle of light was such that
no reflection whatever showed on the immaculate plate glass
that formed the entire front of the house.

A few years ago another garden tour afforded me much
amusement as well as hard work, since I had organized it myself.

We arranged it for the benefit of the Saint-Gaudens Memorial, of which my husband was curator, and were gratified at the unexpectedly heavy sale of tickets. The tour included several pleasant gardens and two of outstanding beauty, one of which was influenced by Italian landscaping. From a marble balustraded terrace, one looked down upon carefully designed borders ablaze with color, while beyond them stretched a green meadow sloping gently to a distant wall of white pine woods. The other garden was quite small but patterned somewhat in the manner of Elizabethan "knots"—very formal, very elegant, every detail perfect. But it was not these attractions that sold our tickets in such profusion. No doubt a few people bought them in the hope that when they walked in the quiet restful garden of Judge Learned Hand they might catch a glimpse of the eminent jurist. But by far the largest number of people pinned their hope on the chance of seeing Maxfield Parrish. Since the only planting I can remember anywhere near Mr. Parrish's house was a mass of common daylilies I could only agree with the crowd that the handsome old gentleman, with his sunburned face, bright blue eyes, and snow-white hair, was indeed a more attractive spectacle than his garden.

Flower shows, although I am an incurable addict, leave me in a jumbled confusion of pleasure and irritation. The inevitable piece of driftwood, with a single spray of gladiolus "echoing" the curve of a branch of the driftwood, and the equally inevitable "fan" of white gladioli, usually designed for altar decoration, sends me scurrying to the house plants, which are not susceptible to arrangement. Horticultural clichés are just as tiresome as verbal ones.

There was one local flower show, however, that sent me away wholly satisfied and happy. The club that sponsored this show

staged it in the rooms. of the town's historical society, where
spindle-legged tables and faded old portraits added charm to
the display of flowers. The club is a member of the state federation of garden clubs, but for this show it did not enter the state
contest with its paraphernalia of judges and rules. The members
simply brought in bouquets from their gardens, and the brilliant
flowers glowed like jewels in the rather dimly lighted rooms.
The casual effect was of course deceptive but all the same ap-
pealing, because each bouquet was obviously the result of someone's affectionate concern rather than the result of compliance
with rules that would net the exhibitor a blue ribbon.

Ordinarily garden clubs rely on arrangements as the backbone
of their flower shows, but to my possibly jaundiced eye the cult
of flower arrangement as practiced in the U.S.A. approaches
the dimensions of a genteel racket overlaid with more than a
smack of pretentiousness.

"Mrs. Blank specializes in arrangements for formal dinners,"
said a member of my own garden club at a meeting one night.
She was one of those advocating the engagement of a certain
lecturer for our next season's program.

I looked around the room. Only a few members had responded
to a hasty summons to reconsider the date of our flower show,
about which some difficulty had arisen, but those present offered
a fair cross section of the club. The date for the flower show was
still unsettled when the lady who specialized in formal dinners
was introduced, but like all meetings this one had wandered off
into irrelevancies. The members present included several office
workers, a trained nurse, two nurses' aides, a high school teacher,
a telephone operator, and the town clerk. The proposed lecturer
would involve the expenditure of hard-earned money.

"How many of you," I asked, "give formal dinners? When I

have people for dinner I cook and serve the meal myself. There's nothing formal about that. You can't have a formal dinner without servants, and there's nary a one among the lot of us."

It would be sentimental to think it touching that such hard working, small-town women should hanker for glamor, higher status, and glittering amenities. These are perfectly sensible women, but very busy ones who can easily be seduced by proposals they have not the time to examine. The notion of flower arrangements for formal dinners can be sold to them as readily as kerosene, dressed up with a trick name, a dazzling container, and a heavy disguise of scent, was sold to them as a superlative cleaning agent by a TV promotion campaign a year or two ago.

If I myself am going to be critical of this sort of concern with flower arrangement I should in all decency admit my indebtedness to one aspect of it that came my way. In a publication by a state federation of garden clubs I found the following announcement: "Annual Federation Flower Show. Don't forget to enter an arrangement at the Annual Meeting Show. . . . One class only—Honoring our State President. Theme—'An interpretive Description of Mary Jane Brown.'"

The fascinating possibilities inherent in this theme have brightened many a tedious trip to the supermarket for me. Since I have never met this person, whose name, of course, is not Mary Jane Brown, my fancy has been free to imagine her as short or tall, fat or thin, soft-spoken or commanding.

If she is a chubby little thing, I muse as I trudge along the village street, perhaps well rounded pompon zinnias, their colors carefully chosen to suggest blond or brunette, as the case might be, could be adequately descriptive. If she is tall and imperious a spike of the large Hosta, flinging its purple trumpets out horizontally, might give the proper strong-arm effect. If she is frilly and gay, ruffled petunias might best serve to evoke her personality. If the state president is a pretty woman with a name like Kelly or Kennedy something might be done with the Bells (belles) of Ireland. I also thought of an arrangement of patience or Patient Lucy, as Impatiens is often politely mistranslated, but dismissed it on the grounds that it was not likely to prove interpretive of a top-flight executive. Love-in-a-mist, bleeding heart, and even widow's-tears offer suggestions which I have still to pursue. But I find I must ration myself in this pleasant pastime. I tend all too easily to become so absorbed that I arrive home minus the detergent or frozen vegetables on which my attention should have been riveted.

Frivolity aside, flower arrangement can be art of a high order, as it is with the Japanese. But by no stretch of the imagination—at least not of mine—can driftwood clichés, formal dinner-table decorations for informal households, and interpretive descriptions of female executives be classified as art. Arrangements based on such ideas displayed at a flower show send me back to my own garden, feeling that I shall be content to stay there for the rest of the summer. Or so I think. But I inevitably succumb to the next show announced in the local paper.

When summer comes to town so do the tourists. Our house stands only a few feet away from one of Vermont's main north-south U.S. highways, and there are times when it seems as if the whole of the United States had decided to make a summer-visit to New England. License plates from Idaho and Utah, Oregon and Iowa, Arkansas and Arizona flash past. Sometimes the out-of-town cars draw up to the curb, passengers emerge to stretch their legs and to tell me across the fence about their own gardens back home.

With summer come visiting family and friends. Every one

talks of grandchildren. Life in a quiet New England village expands to embrace the world when summer comes to town.

Familiar faces from far away, the roaring traffic, and the sense of a whole, mobile, wide-flung continent, all these would have seemed incredible to the man whose pleasant phrase I have borrowed as the title and theme of this chapter. When summer comes to town, as Bald the Anglo-Saxon physician wrote in his leech-book, you may gather this herb or that. Repetition did not bother Bald, so the phrase recurs as this conscientious and hard-working doctor set down his prescriptions and medical observations almost exactly a thousand years ago.

When Bald wrote the word "town" one wonders what sort of cluster of huts and hovels rose to his mind's eye, set perhaps beside a quiet river or backed by the dense forest that covered most of England in his day. Barring an occasional horse or oxcart, his means of transportation for making his professional rounds were his own two feet. But the herbs he used still star English meadows, and many have migrated to this country to brighten our own when summer comes to town.

11

Putting House Plants out to Pasture

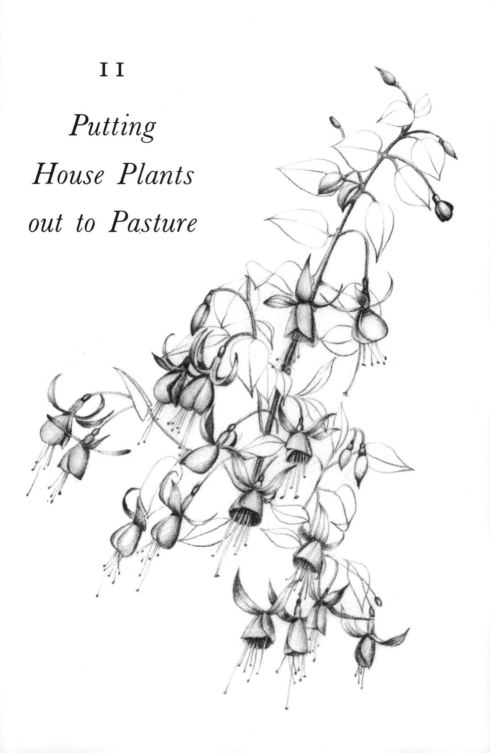

No account of gardening on Main Street would be complete without some mention of the house plants brought out of doors to summer there. Not all house plants lend themselves to this treatment, but there are quite a few that can be put out to pasture, as it were, like cattle. They seem to enjoy the chance to stretch themselves and grow as much as the beasts do. (This simile comes naturally to a Vermonter because up to the last census, when the balance shifted a little, the state has boasted for decades a larger population of cows than of people.)

Carried out into the garden in their pots, fuchsias and shrimpplants, among others, flower more readily outdoors than they do inside. Wax begonias, on the other hand, are tired plants by spring and badly in need of a rest. I knock mine out of their pots, divide them, and cut the growth back to a mere inch or two. These shabby remnants of past glories are then planted inconspicuously here and there in shady places. I often forget their existence when my attention is focussed on the succession of summer bloom. Then, unexpectedly, a flash of pink or red or white reminds me that the begonias are getting on their feet in preparation for the long winter ahead.

House plants are an absorbing preoccupation with many gardeners, but nowhere more so than here in northern New England, where the summers are so very short and the winters so very long.

Many New England housewives are highly skilled indoor gardeners, and I have met several who cherished ancestral plants handed down from their mothers or even from their grandmothers. Now increasing numbers of newcomers like myself are becoming enthusiastic practitioners of this form of gardening. There must be thousands of us—women whose husbands have retired and who have come from cities and suburbs to spend the rest of their lives in rural areas. House plants, most of us promptly decide, are definitely part of such living. Like all novices we start out with the illusion that the care and feeding of house plants are easy matters and that a few minutes of attention each day will yield us masses of bloom indoors, no matter how far below zero it may be outside.

Nothing could be further from the truth. It takes time and experience to learn the tricks of the trade. Disappointments alternate with satisfactions. Yet, once caught up in the fascination of growing things when all the world is white with snow, the new indoor gardener persists in spite of difficulties and frustrations that are legion. At least so it was in my case.

Take the African violet for instance—and so far as I am concerned anyone may take it. There are few plants that I covet so much, few that I have worked over so hard, but they firmly refuse to bloom for me.

This, I submit, is not for want of trying. Eight years ago I was given half a dozen husky young plants by a friend whose own plants produced, by actual count, forty to forty-five flowers at a time. Purple, lavender and almost true blue, pink and white, double and single, African violets on their white wire stand and scattered around on desk or tables made her living room an exciting place to enter. Where the walls of that room were not covered with books they were paneled with pine. A big fireplace faced wide French windows on the west, and a huge pink and tan Kermanshah rug covered nearly the whole floor. African violets lit that softly blond room as if with colored lights.

I followed the careful directions this friend gave me, but all in vain. Then she moved away and I began on my own. It would be tedious if I tried to give a blow-by-blow account of my experience with African violets, but I can at least summarize it.

I had two excellent books on house plants and I acquired one devoted entirely to the cultivation of African violets. Then I clipped from *Horticulture* and various other garden magazines such articles as I thought might be helpful. Nor did I stick strictly to "book larnin." There are scores of women in our village and the nearby countryside whose plants are justifiably their pride, and of all I met I enquired the secret of their success.

To say that the result was maddening is to put it mildly. Not that I think that a single woman tried to mislead me. On the contrary, they were generous with advice and eager to explain how they had achieved such magnificent results, but their methods proved to be wildly dissimilar, not to say confusing.

"How often do you water them?" I asked one friend whose plants taunted me with their exuberant bloom.

"Oh I don't know," she answered. "I suppose about once a week. Never until the top soil feels dusty to my fingers—well dried out. And of course I keep them shaded."

"How often do you water them?" I repeated to another neighbor whose plants, loaded with blossoms, stretched along the sill of a big south window, each plant in its little aluminum pie plate.

"Late afternoon every day of the week," she replied briskly.

"I fill each of those little pie plates with warm water as full as the plate will hold. The plants should never dry out and they seem to like all the sun they can get."

In sun or shade, moist or dry, African violets will bloom, I am more than half convinced, only for those people whom they like.

"My grandmother used to say that you have to talk to house plants," a country neighbor once told me. "She said that you had to love them and let them know that you loved them." An old wives' tale? It would be a bold man or woman who would volunteer a dogmatic negative today. So many old wives' tales, so many fantastic flights into science fiction have turned out to have a sound basis in scientific fact that we have become skeptical of traditional certainties. I, for one, would not be in the least surprised to learn that a series of scientific experiments had demonstrated that there is a subtle relationship between plants and human beings measurable in their responses to each other. In any case, the response of African violets to me is adverse. I am driven to the conclusion that they do not like me.

Any gardener who has played the old association-of-ideas game knows that if the term "house plant" is given, nine players out of ten will reply "African violets." For that reason I have disposed of this problem child of the indoor garden before reporting on a useful treatment for some of its better balanced inhabitants.

I have already mentioned the shrimp-plant, which is one of these, but since it is a favorite of mine I should like to elaborate a little.

When I take a shrimp-plant outdoors I sink it, still in its pot, in a shady place on the far side of the pool. Then I prune it back, keeping several of the longest cuttings. I strip the lower leaves from these, stick the bared stems into any convenient spot, and, as in the case of wax begonias, usually forget all about them. Not always, but sometimes I have been rewarded with sturdy new plants to pot and carry indoors for the winter.

Alternanthera is another house plant that I find is all the better for a summer in the garden. Until we came to live in New England I had never so much as heard of this particular plant, but here it is so common that I was surprised to find how difficult it was to track down what it is. When I had found out, it seemed a pity that this useful and decorative ornament of so many country kitchens and parlors had never been christened with anything less formidable than its generic name. "Ruby Glory" would be suitable, though corny, and at least both manageable and descriptive. Ruby something it should be, for the whole plant, stems as well as the kidney-shaped leaves, is reminiscent of the finest ruby-red stained glass. Glass comes to mind instead of an actual ruby, because the plant is at its best on a window sill with a background of snow behind it and winter sunlight streaming through that glowing color.

Yet for all its spectacular appearance, Alternanthera is robust, undemanding, and practically indestructible. I carry a plant outdoors when the weather has grown warm, knock it out of its pot, and plant it. It doesn't seem to matter where—in sun or shade, in wet ground or dry. The only care I take is to make sure that I do not put it where its dominating red will do violence to some nearby color scheme, especially since it grows stout and tall as the summer advances. In September I take advantage of this stout growth. I cut a good bouquet of five- or six-inch sprigs, put them in water and a few weeks later pot as many well rooted cuttings as I think I shall need in winter. Frost disposes of the original plant for me.

Geraniums, too, profit by a summer in the garden. The dishevelled plants that one carries outdoors after a long winter look as if they were going from dormancy to death—and some do. Those, however, that survive suddenly shoot out new growth and sometimes gay sprigs of bloom before the summer is over. These latter, if one is counting on winter bloom, must be pinched off immediately. Otherwise, all the sun they can get and not too much water are all that geraniums seem to demand.

For the first few years of my gardening on Main Street I used to carry my amaryllis outdoors in summer. This is considered advisable by the authorities, but I failed to follow all the details of their directions and so had my trouble for nothing. The bulbs need careful feeding during their growing period, and this I neglected. My garden as a whole gets its bone meal and fertilizer dug or scratched in, spring and fall, before and after its season of bloom. To carry on a special program of feeding no more than two or four plants at the busiest time of the year was beyond me.

This is one excuse for failure, but there is also another. I have country neighbors who carry their amaryllis over from year to year with great success, and I cherish a conviction that they manage to do this without anything like the attention to the bulbs that is recommended by the experts. I have never gone into the matter deeply, but my impression is that they "just let the leaves keep on growing during the summer, cut them back in the fall, and then put the pots in the cellar until spring." It sounds simple and easy, but it does not work for me.

Then, too, the fact that I force my bulbs with bottom heat,

as I shall describe later, leaves them in no condition to flower the following year. Experts can, I believe, bring such bulbs back to normal growth by a long-term regime of care and coddling, but such niceties are beyond my capacity. I now follow the extravagant practice of buying new bulbs each year and salve my conscience by turning them over, after they have bloomed, to a friend who has a greenhouse and a nursery business. She is willing to fuss with them—and I wish her well.

There is a modified version of putting house plants out to pasture that is denied me because we have no porch, front or back. Many of my country neighbors bring most of their house plants out to the porch in summer. I have seen African violets, gloxinias, calla-lily-leaved begonias, and many others expand into exuberant bloom in the fresh air, while at the same time they are protected from the extremes of summer weather. There, too, one finds such summer-flowering bulbs and tubers as gloriosa lilies and achimenes, which are not suited to the garden, at least not to northern gardens like ours. The achimenes haunt me, for I have seen magnificent specimens flourishing on many a modest country porch, but since I have no place to put them I can only gaze at them with a longing that I know should be subdued.

It is undoubtedly just as well that we have no porch. As it is, even the few house plants that I carry out into the garden cost me a little something in time. And after the weather gets warm, time is a precious commodity. One always plans to hoard it with care for the most pressing chores, but, as summer advances, much of it just drifts away while one wanders around the garden, enjoying a successful color scheme here or planning to improve another yonder. Gardener's eyes always look to the future. More primroses will be needed next spring, more Browallia next summer. So by and large, my house plants have to fend for themselves, and I am grateful to the small new shrimp-plants and wax begonias that flourish in inconspicuous corners.

In a garden as small as mine, where pasturage for house plants is not extensive—and mine is measurable in inches—I content myself with a few and those only the most undemanding.

12

The Saddest Time
of the Year

"I always think that this is the saddest time of the year."

A fat lugubrious voice, dripping with sentimental overtones, wafted across the fence toward where I knelt planting daffodils. I made some noncommittal reply, less from lack of conviction than from lack of eagerness to pursue the subject with a neighbor ever ready to dwell on the darker side of life.

When she had waddled away I sat back on my heels and took a look at the bulb in my hand. It was vibrant with life—its shiny outer coat a warm chestnut brown, three offsets still clinging to the mother bulb. Six months hence, barring my own carelessness or some natural catastrophe, it would send up the flowers of the Narcissus La Riante, its pointed white petals flaring around its shallow, ruffled cup of deep yellow. There was nothing sad about it. Nor, so far as I was concerned, was there anything sad about the season itself even on that bleak November day.

I love Vermont winters, but most native Vermonters complain bitterly that the snow and cold last far too long. Some years ago a friend of mine asked John Dewey, then over ninety and basking in the February warmth of Florida, to what he attributed his longevity. "Anyone," he told her, "who can survive a Vermont childhood can live forever."

Winters were rugged indeed in Vermont a century ago, but now that their worst hardships have been overcome by modern technology, I could look forward to the one ahead with pleasure. There would probably be snow within a week or ten days of that bulb planting, I reflected, and there would be snow on the ground until April, possibly until well into April. But meantime the bulbs would be safe in the frozen ground and the coming winter, white and quiet, looked far from sad to me. My husband would be busy at his easel, I at my typewriter. There would be friends to see, fires to scent the living room, and all the flowers and gardens of the world to explore between the covers of books.

My garden is richer and more colorful because of my reading. Tulips flaunt a special gaiety against the background of that fantastic financial affair that Wilfrid Blunt describes in *Tulipomania*. E. H. Wilson's account of a mountain meadow on the Chinese-Tibetan border resplendent with regal lilies gives added dignity to my own gold-throated trumpets blaring their silent music over a picket fence along a New England village street. The Paisley patterns of many small garden pinks evoke memories of the Flemish and French Protestant weavers who fled from persecution on the Continent to England and Scotland. There they eased their poverty and homesickness by breeding, among many other flowers, the sweet-scented little pinks, whose patterns often suggested those of the textiles on their looms. The single auricula growing beside my pool was planted there as an affectionate reminder of that most beguiling of botanists, Charles de l'Ecluse, who first brought this alpine primrose into European gardens. In *Gardener's Tribute* Richardson Wright has left us a brief but lively account of this "prince of descriptive botanists."

To the anticipated pleasures of the coming winter—friends, fires, and books, not to mention house plants—"the saddest time of the year" also ushers in the appearance of the jauntiest and most incredible flower of my acquaintance.

"What is that pink thing growing in your garden, Buckie?" asked a friend who had dropped in for tea on a January afternoon when the garden, like all of our world, lay white under a thick blanket of snow.

"A chewing-gum wrapper," I answered promptly, speaking from experience.

Alice brushed this idea aside, so we went to a south window where we could look down toward "the pink thing" that she continued to insist was growing there. And so it was—but in the plural, not the singular, for we could see from our elevation three or four Christmas roses, even the soft dimness of their pink dramatic in the midst of the whiteness around them.

Vivid pink Christmas roses, bright against the snow, are a familiar sight to gardeners who brood over the glossy color advertisements in their garden magazines. Pink and white are a color combination that suggests delicacy to most of us, and even, by association, a certain fragility. No suggestion could be more misleading. There is nothing whatever either delicate or fragile about the tough little Christmas rose. It is rugged enough, in all truth, to bloom not only through the light snows of a temperate climate and through the light snows of late November here, but it can also bloom in the bitter cold and heavy snowfall of a northern New England winter.

There may be vivid pink varieties of *Helleborus niger,* but the few pink ones that I have produce flowers that are a dim pink, fading with age to a dull crimson. Most of my Christmas roses, however, are white.

It is a triumphant moment when the plants reach the climax of their bloom early in December and again late in March or very early April. From a thick rosette of dark, evergreen leaves, many of them lying close to the ground, rise masses of white flowers and, in my garden, a few pink ones. Each flower on its sturdy bare stem, about eight inches tall, is a two-inch replica of my huge, single white peonies, to which they are closely related. The sepals curve gently into a shallow cup ablaze with the gold of their pistils and stamens.

Christmas roses came into my life through the kindness of a neighbor—one of those with whom I had often chatted across the fence. On a dark November day Miss Andersen arrived at our house bearing a big bouquet of flowers that I recognized instantly, although I had never seen that kind before. To say that I was delighted was putting it mildly.

The bouquet was so large that I was concerned lest she had robbed herself but she reassured me. She had so many Christmas roses, she told me, that she could easily spare these. Thirty years before a friend of her father's had given him a few plants. They had flourished and grown and spread. There was now a large patch of ground near the house so covered with flowering plants that no one would suspect that any flowers had been picked.

The following spring this generous neighbor reappeared at

our house, carrying a good-sized carton in which she displayed a wealth of shining, dark green leaves covering a great treasure of plants.

"You were so excited about the Christmas roses that I brought you last fall," said Miss Andersen, "that I thought you might like to have these." Then she went on to explain that she was moving to Connecticut, had carried a great many of her plants to her garden there, had sent some to her brother in Tennessee, and now wondered if I would like to have the rest. Would I!

In addition to my appreciation of this fabulous present, there was the pleasure of knowing the background of my new plants. For more than three decades they had been the pride of a whole family. It was good to know that many of them would continue in this role, even in alien states, and that those remaining in Vermont were consigned to my care.

Miss Andersen could not give me much help as to where to put my plants. She thought they would grow almost anywhere, but admitted that she understood they were hard to establish. As a help to solving this problem she had brought along a generous supply of the earth in which they had grown and she advised me to tuck the familiar soil around their roots when I planted them.

After she had gone I examined my treasure. Besides a small clump of four or five plants, there were three big clumps of probably twelve to fifteen plants each, their roots tightly interlaced. Scattered about in the loose soil in the box were several single plants that I was especially glad to see, as they showed me the habit of growth of Helleborus. Each plant had a forked root about as long and much thinner than my fingers. From these rose several tough-stemmed leaves which, as the flowers did later, proclaimed their kinship with peonies. I gave away these separate plants by two's and three's and concentrated on my four clumps.

Winter sun and summer shade, I learned from my garden dictionaries, was what the plants required and winter sun and summer shade were conditions my garden could supply. Where the path that curves around the apple tree ends against the back border, I set the small clump to one side of the path in the triangle with the astilbe and put the larger clump on the apple-tree side of the path. Not only the apple tree but also the elm in the yard below the garden supplied the plants with shade all summer and then in winter, after the trees had lost their leaves, let the sunlight reach them.

With the two larger clumps I took a chance. If the flowers actually did bloom in cold weather, not to mention through the snow, I wanted them where they could be seen from indoors. I set one clump opposite each of the windows that flank our front door—a living room window on one side, a dining room window on the other. I dug the plants in close to the picket fence and less than five feet from the windows. There they get no morning sun at all. For a brief hour toward noon direct sunlight falls on them, and after that there are the striped sunshine and shadow that come to them through the fence. It was a happy choice, for they have flourished mightily. Just as I had hoped, I can stand at that living room window, an open fire snapping in the background, and look out at a glory of white and gold flowers blooming improbably in the snow.

The first time I had seen my Christmas roses in bloom had been in the November before my friend Alice discovered the "pink thing" and about six months after Miss Andersen had given them to me. Not only was I delighted to have found flowers blooming near the apple tree, but at the time I had a special use for them. My husband and I were going to Cambridge to spend Thanksgiving with our "law-kin." ("Law-kin," for those unacquainted with this convenient, old-fashioned term, are one's children's in-laws.) Flowers gathered in the snow well north of Boston should make an acceptable house present. I carried the hearth brush along with me when I went outdoors and gently brushed the snow away so that I could cut the flowers. My bouquet was not as munificent as the one Miss Andersen had brought me, but it was warmly welcomed and served as an excellent conversation piece.

At the time of the November harvesting I had noted two things. Although I had had to brush the snow away in order to cut the flowers, it was much thinner over the plants than elsewhere in the garden. I concluded that the heat generated by their growth explains the miracle of their winter bloom. But why any plant should continue to grow in near-zero, zero, and sub-zero weather I do not know. All other perennials retire into respectable dormancy under such conditions.

The other thing I had noticed was that there were plenty of buds coming along close to the ground. A couple of weeks later, in December, I went out again and gathered flowers in the snow. This time they decorated our dining room table. They last a long time in water.

That first year I had Christmas roses in November and December as well as the pink ones in January. This sequence inspired me to find out if there might, by some incredible chance, be more flowers in February. This time I needed a shovel as well as the hearth brush. I heaved quite a respectable heap of snow off the spot where plants grew near the fence and opposite the living room window and then brushed more away. There were three half-open buds to be picked and carried indoors.

Much later that February we had a heavy thaw. Icicles melting from the roof nearly cleared the snow from one of the clumps of Christmas roses by the fence and then, when the inevitable cold returned, covered the plants with a thick glaze of ice. Through this I was able to make out not only the dark green leaves but also a few little white balls, which were buds, firmly frozen to the ground. Not even Christmas roses can survive such treatment. Although they made a valiant effort as soon as the sun could touch them, those buds browned off before they could get clear of the ground. But others, not quite mature enough to show through the ice, took their place, and I had flowers before March was over.

This gave me great satisfaction. Years ago when I built my rock garden on our New York place I had used Louise Beebe Wilder's *Adventures in My Garden and Rock Garden* as a sort of Bible. In this book Mrs. Wilder admitted to her thwarted ambition to pick something in her garden every month in the year. In that garden, about thirty-five miles up the Hudson from New York City, she had been able to gather an occasional Johnny or a spray of myrtle even in December and January. But February had defeated her. I had tried to emulate that distinguished gardener and had had much the same experience in a garden not many miles from the one about which she was writing. Yet here in Vermont, in a much more rigorous climate, I have gathered flowers in my garden every month in the year—thanks to Christmas roses.

Most garden books start with the excitements of spring and

continue until they reach a finale in the drab and colorless chores of fall. The story of my garden carries on from there—carries on through snow and ice, through temperatures down to ten and twenty degrees below zero, until April comes to bring the first blue squills and the sumptuous purple and gold and white of crocus. My small garden on Main Street goes full circle without beginning or end.

I3

Winter Bloom
Indoors

When we bought our house on Main Street I looked forward with special interest to house plants, to masses of bloom everywhere all winter long. But I counted without my artist husband.

"Have all the plants you want," he said to me one morning as we stood in the empty living room where carpenters were at work on the book shelves, "but I don't want the windows of this room cluttered with them."

I, who had been doing just exactly that in my mind, said nothing. At the time I grasped only dimly what he meant, but later, when I had explored the collections of a number of indoor gardeners, I understood his objection. I have seen many a window sill packed to the last inch with plants, in space so precious that they were crowded together helter-skelter without regard to size, shape, or color. My sympathies were torn between those indoor gardeners who could not bear to part with a single plant and my husband's desire to keep the general pattern of our living room serene and devoid of clutter. When I announced that I would curb my limitless enthusiasm for anything that would grow anywhere and also my intention to use house plants strictly as decoration, we both agreed it would be nice to have flowers growing in the living room.

Oddly enough I was to discover that the very limitations that this decision imposed added both interest and pleasure to my indoor gardening. I would find myself looking at a collection of, say, wax begonias, not only to enjoy their forms and colors, but also to choose one or more of them as components of a design on a window sill.

Our living room, twenty-four feet long by fourteen wide, is entered near the front windows, which face west. These windows, unlike the others in the room, are very tall, their sills only a few inches above the floor. In the long south wall is an open fireplace, with windows to the right and left of it. The narrow east end of the room is covered entirely with book shelves except in the center, where the shelves have been built around a single window. Since this window is sunk in the shelves, it has an exceptionally generous sill, the original one extended by the width of the shelves surrounding it.

The sills of the two south windows were easily widened a few inches, but the front ones, reaching almost to the floor remained a problem until I remembered the andirons that had lain so long in our attic.

Years before a friend, who had been dismantling a big house, presented us with a pair of andirons wildly unsuited to our scale of living. They were so tall and stately that they should have graced a baronial hall. The two twisted iron straps that formed their uprights opened out at the top into four, which curved to make a bowl-like arrangement; this last was finished with a flat, iron ring. The ideal pot-holder!

The village blacksmith—the last of his trade in this locality— cut off all but a few inches of the business ends of our andirons and, with very little adjustment, the stubs were fitted on and fastened to the low sills of those problem windows. Thus we achieved, in the center of each of these, a slim handsome support for a good-sized potted plant.

"How perfectly damned awful!" exclaimed an English friend of ours when he first surveyed our newly installed pot-holders. "I have been looking for a pair of wine warmers for years." It had never occurred to either of us that our andirons had been designed to cradle bottles of red wine warming before the embers.

Once the room was finished, it was painted, walls, woodwork, andirons, and all, a greyed-down powder blue, much the same color as British flying-corps' uniforms. The east window was left bare among its surrounding book shelves, but the other four were flanked, from floor to ceiling, with white corduroy curtains lined with rose-colored glazed chintz. These, then, were the spaces and colors with which I would have to deal.

Of all the plants that have gone into our wine warmers the most exciting have been amaryllis—Salmon Joy, Apple Blossom, Margaret Rose, and Love's Desire, among others. I buy my bulbs from a dealer in Baton Rouge, Louisiana, at about half the price I would pay for a potted specimen from some of the Eastern nurserymen. Furthermore I can get named varieties chosen from a descriptive catalogue, instead of having to select nothing more definite than "pink," "red," or "white" among the already potted offerings.

A pair of bulbs of Salmon Joy were the first I ordered, and when they bloomed they both amazed and disappointed me. The flowers were magnificent, each eight inches across and of a fine form and texture. But their color was an orangy red. I am a very literal-minded person, and the word "Salmon," used as a color term, suggests to me only the deep warm pink of the fish's flesh. Since then I have chosen only flowers whose descriptions guaranteed a true pink, from the deep shade of Margaret Rose to the pale tint of Apple Blossom.

Love's Desire lies somewhere between the two and is all that its name suggests. A few steps away, the flower appears to be a delicate pink, but on close inspection one sees that it is white, heavily veined with the warm color. From its pale green throat long white stamens emerge, clubbed at the ends with old-gold anthers. A strong scape lifts two or four flowers nearly two feet above the bulb so that, given such height plus that of the pot and the wine warmer in which it stands, the huge flowers are not far below human eye level. To enter our living room and come all unexpectedly face to face, as it were, with Love's Desire in bloom is an experience.

"Love's Desire?" exclaimed a friend when this had happened to her. "Love's Desire," she repeated more slowly. "Satisfied? or unsatisfied?—Oh, satisfied, of course."

In Dr. Hamilton P. Traub's fine book on amaryllis I picked up a hint that the bulbs could be brought into bloom more quickly than usual if bottom heat was supplied. Mine, after I pot them, go, as a routine matter, into our cellar until the first tips of leaves begin to show. Then I carry them up to the bedroom floor and put them on a pebble tray near a window. There they stay until the buds are almost ready to open, when they are brought downstairs for display in the wine warmers.

One fall my bulbs arrived late, and, as I potted them, I was sorry that there appeared to be no chance of any blossoms by Christmas. Then, remembering Dr. Traub's suggestion, I started a new regime. When I went upstairs in the evening to change for dinner, I would carry the two pots into the bathroom, water them, and put them down in a dim corner on a floor register.

Later, when we went to bed, the thermostat was always turned down a little, but the heat thus applied was sufficient. Both plants provided me with a glorious display throughout the holidays. I had brought them into bloom in three weeks!

There are times when our pot holders contain nothing more spectacular than well shaped foliage plants, but in their season cyclamen, Easter lilies, and Star of Bethlehem serve me well. Especially the latter. In my Maryland childhood, Star of Bethlehem was the common name given the little spring bulb *Ornithogalum umbellatum,* but here in Vermont the name means *Campanula isophylla,* which is a cherished house plant in this part of the world. Some of my neighbors carry it over from year to year, but one woman, who grows plants by the score for sale, tells me that she cuts back all her remaining plants in the late fall and discards them. She then grows a whole new crop from the cuttings thus collected. The big pots these plants need take up so much room on my pebble tray that I don't try to carry them over but buy new ones each summer. From late July until into November they shake out long white bridal veils of bloom in front windows.

The masses of flowers that I had anticipated indoors during my first winter in New England have never materialized, but like all persistent indoor gardeners, I have had my moments of triumph. One came on a day in February when all our world was white out of doors and the thermometer registered twenty degrees below zero.

Love's Desire stood in ostentatious arrogance in the wine warmers at our front windows.

In those windows looking south, Hattie's begonia put on a satisfactory but much more modest display. This plant is a shrubby little thing, a tuberous begonia, whose growth at that time was about eight or ten inches high. On translucent red stems it boasted a wealth of finely cut, maple-like leaves and, on that February morning, pale pink flowers fluttered all over the plants like flocks of small butterflies. I had put a specimen of this begonia against the dark green of Christmas cactus, not then in bloom, at the center of each of those two windows. To the right and left of the frivolous pink thing were low pans holding cuttings recently made from an old *Rhœo discolor,* their shiny dark green rosettes making a pleasant contrast with the mat green of the cactus.

I had named Hattie's begonia after the friend who had originally given me cuttings from her much larger plant, but I was anxious to know which begonia Hattie's was, and I was equally curious about the identity of still another begonia that my neighbors call A Yard of Roses. The latter, according to Bailey's *Standard Cyclopedia of Horticulture,* turns out to be Gloire de Lorraine (*Begonia dregei* x *Begonia socotrana*). No plant I know has more right to be called the glory of something or other than this one has, but all the same I find the New England name even more graphic.

Hattie's begonia still eludes me. No less an authority than the Liberty Hyde Bailey Hortorium at Cornell has informed me that I may as well go right on calling Hattie's begonia just that. It is a hybrid but no one has been able to identify its parentage.

Moses-in-the-bulrushes is the name commonly used in New England for *Rhœo discolor*—to my way of thinking, the most appropriate of many names given to this plant. Very early in the spring, narrow bracts, shaped like canoes, each only a little more than an inch long, appear at points where a leaf joins the main stem. These bracts open out to reveal one, two, rarely three, tiny Moseses. The triangular shape of the little white flowers suggests their kinship to Tradescantia, to which it is indeed related. The flowers themselves are so small that if one were flattened on a dime a thin rim of silver would still show.

At the far end of the room, to turn back to that February morning, the window set among the book shelves finished that winter display with a fine flourish. The central feature of the arrangement there was my treasured Yard of Roses, its pot set in a white stemmed bowl high enough to permit the cascade of vivid rose-pink blossoms to show to their best advantage. From a tight cushion of bright green foliage a great many lax stems emerged, each tipped with only two flowers, but when these fade and fall the stem lengthens and two more flowers appear. There are so many stems of so many varying lengths that the plant becomes a fountain of rose-colored flowers.

Nor did a vibrant red detract in the least from that dominating pink. I had put three plants in a row very close to the window itself, an Alternanthera in each corner and an Apostle-plant in the center just behind the Yard of Roses. The ruby glow that thin winter sunlight imparts to Alternanthera would have been too strong if the plants had not been largely masked by the figures of two ladies who live on that window sill. These are a pair of Parian marble statuettes, sweetly sentimental Victorian versions of Greek goddesses, modestly swathed in voluminous robes and with coiffures of neatly flowing tresses.

The Apostle-plant takes its familiar name from the fact that its sword-shaped leaves are almost always twelve in number. They spread against that window, as they always do, in a beautifully symmetrical fan and, on that particular morning, three of their flowers appeared on the leaves, behind and above my Yard of Roses.

In defiance of all the rules, the flowers of Neomarica—to give the Apostle-plant its formal name, which is often shortened to Marica—emerge from the leaves themselves. The watchful indoor gardener will note that toward the middle of winter a leaf will thicken at a certain point well above half its height. The thickening pushes outward in the form of a green nub, from which two little leaves unfold, a budded stem between them. After the flowers have faded this excrescence on the side of the leaf is allowed to grow until it looks sturdy enough to be broken from the parent leaf. Then, if potted and cared for, the nub becomes a rhizome, more and stronger leaves shoot out, and a new plant is on its way to maturity. In nature, where there is no watchful human to act as midwife, the weight of the flowering shoot carries the leaf down to the ground. In the rich soil of the tropical African or South American jungles the embryonic rhizome quickly develops roots to anchor the young plant; then the parent leaf can break free and snap back into its place in the fan.

All this I find very interesting, but the flowers are sheer miracle. Like other members of the iris family, to which this plant belongs, the blossoms appear in three-segment form. Three zinc-white petals flare horizontally and are about four inches across. Three others, a deep almost dark blue, curl in the center, and all the segments have long white claws banded with a rich red brown. These flowers open at the first touch of the morning sun and are gone by the time it sets, but ephemeral as they are, they are well worth the long year of waiting.

In front of the Yard of Roses and well below their cascade of bloom, I had set a low pan of pale pink fairy lilies. These charming natives of Florida are sometimes also called rain lilies because, when growing out of doors, they respond so readily and gratefully to every shower.

To add a little more green to the varying red and pink I had put little pots of tiny, shrubby wax begonia cuttings to the right and left of the fairy lilies and in front of the white draperies of the Victorian ladies. The pinks and greens, the red and white, with the dark blue centers of the Marica above the rest, were all any indoor gardener could ask.

That was a good day, but it is not often that I can get so many things to bloom at one time in one room. I describe it not only because gardeners are seldom afflicted with modesty, but also because it illustrates how I avoided a clutter of plants in our living room and sometimes succeeded in making a well patterned display in each window.

More recently I have added spring flowering bulbs to my stock in trade of amaryllis, Marica, Christmas cactus, Moses-in-the-bulrushes, Alternanthera, and a wide variety of begonias, which includes a beguiling miniature *rex*.

I had tried spring-flowering bulbs in my early days of indoor gardening, but without much success until I realized the extraordinary facilities for growing them that I had at hand and had been neglecting. Right under my nose, as it were, were the two necessary conditions they must have to produce flowers—a cold dark place in which to start growth and a cool light place in which to continue their growth until the buds are up and well formed.

My most valuable facility is provided by a defect of the insulation in the east wall of our kitchen. Because of this, the pipes under my kitchen sink sometimes freeze when the temperature outdoors drops to twenty or more degrees below zero. We have been planning for years to have the necessary repairs made, but we never remember to do so until catastrophe overtakes us, always, of course, when weather conditions are too severe to make such work possible. Now it will never be made as long as I have my strength!

To the left of the kitchen sink stretches a counter with two drawers under it. Below the drawers is a roomy compartment, hitherto used for oddments, that gets the same blast of cold that affects the water pipes nearby. But a little freezing never hurts spring-flowering bulbs, and they flourish in the average 45 degrees that the compartment ordinarily supplies.

After trying ordinary potting soil with and without a generous addition of sand and small gravel, I turned to perlite and vermiculite. Crocus do best in the latter, set almost on the surface and kept thoroughly wet. The roots of all but the tiniest daffodil need small pebbles to anchor them—just pebbles in water since the bulbs themselves have already stored their own nourishment and need only moisture.

The tiniest daffodil I mentioned bears the apt botannical name *Narcissus minimus*. I grow mine in perlite in a stemmed glass affair whose bowl is about six inches wide and two deep. It holds nearly two dozen bulbs. The plant consists of a few leaves like narrow blades of grass two inches high from among which emerges a yellow trumpet daffodil—King Alfred himself, no less—just one inch long! Even *en masse* this midget has little display value to offer—just sheer joy.

Narcissus minor and another six-inch dwarf, a bicolor called Little Beauty, provide our living room with much needed touches of yellow. Friends and neighbors who see these flowers stand breathless before their premature spring splendor.

As all gardeners know, an ordinary crocus corm sends up only a single flower. What many do not know is that the specie, *Crocus chrysanthus,* does much better. Each corm produces from three to six flowers. I once had sixteen colored buds and full blown blossoms at one time in a six-by-three-inch pan that held only five corms.

Crocus chrysanthus, Snow Bunting, is white; E. P. Bowles yellow; *Tomasinianus,* Ruby Giant, warm dark purple; Princess Beatrix white, deeply edged with purple; and my favorite, *sieberi,* is lavender with a yellow throat. If planted late in November or early in December and never allowed to get dry, these crocuses will bloom in about eight weeks.

A New England winter holds no terrors for the dedicated gardener—only opportunities for experiment, some inevitable failures, and many joys.

14

"The Yellow or Orenge Tawnie Gilloflower"

Ghosts walk in most gardens. Usually they are called up by sentiment. Every spring I carry a cluster of pansies and lilies of the valley to the secretary of a friend of mine because, on her way to work, she often pauses by the fence to remark that her mother grew and loved pansies and lilies of the valley. A local businessman frequently stops to make the same remark about the morning-glories that festoon the trellis over our front door.

My ghosts are less personal ones—a valued business acquaintance, three men I never saw, and a farmer-florist who, all unconsciously and because I provided him with an audience,

stimulated my childhood interest in the flowering world. None of my family were gardeners, so I have no sentimental memories of my mother or grandmother bending over the plants they tended.

The first ghost who I think may like to walk in my garden came late into my life. Ellen Shipman had already made a distinguished name for herself in the world of gardening when I first met her as one of the trustees of the Saint-Gaudens Memorial, to which my husband had come as curator. In her young days she had known Saint-Gaudens well and had helped Mrs. Saint-Gaudens lay out the gardens which still add so much beauty to the country place in New Hampshire where much of the sculptor's work was done.

Some years after Mrs. Shipman's death, when I was writing *Her Garden Was Her Delight,* I planned two chapters which never appeared in print. One was to have been about rock gardens, featuring Louise Beebe Wilder, and the other about Ellen Shipman, who, if not actually the first woman landscape architect in this country, was certainly one of the first and best. She laid out some of the gardens at the New York Botanical Garden in the Bronx, and there are famous gardens in Grosse Pointe, Michigan, and in New Orleans which were her work. By any standard she deserves a place among women who have influenced our modern gardens, and I was especially sorry to leave her out, not only on that account but because I had come to have both admiration and affection for her. But fate was against me. What my surgeon considered a brilliantly successful operation for cataract had the ironic result of depriving me of all ability to do further research.

During the last years of her life Mrs. Shipman's own garden became a wild tangle of vivid bloom. I remember especially a flaming mass of phlox over which rose the steel-blue balls of the globe-thistle. In the well cultivated soil plants had spread and multiplied with an extravagance so exuberant as to be beyond the control of two very old people—Mrs. Shipman herself, and her gardener. But one could walk along the brick-edged paths cushioned with pine needles and follow the pleasant pattern of the beds and borders.

After Mrs. Shipman's death I, like other friends and neighbors, wanted something from her garden to plant in my own. Now if her shade does not care to haunt the wreckage that was once her garden it may be pleased to find in mine, among Rosy Wing tulips, the sky-blue trumpets of the Virginia cowslips she had originally planted a great many years ago.

Three other professional gardeners, long dead, may like to haunt my garden not only because I grow their particular flower there but because I so often think of them when I tend it. John Tradescant was gardener to Charles I of England. After the king lost his head, John's son, John, who had finished his apprenticeship under his father, made the long and dangerous voyage to the colony of Virginia. He went ostensibly to collect and study strange new American plants, but perhaps also to escape the civil war that ravaged his homeland. He returned and eventually became gardener to Charles II after the Restoration. A third John, son of the second and grandson of the first, followed in his progenitors' footsteps but died young while still an apprentice. All three lie buried in Lambeth Churchyard in London, their graves marked by a stone that carries a verse celebrating their work as gardeners.

> Know, stranger, ere thou pass beneath this stone
> Lye JOHN TRADESCANT, grandsire, father, son;

The last dyed in his spring, the other two
Liv'd till they had travell'd art and nature through;

Both gardeners to the ROSE AND LILY QUEEN,
Transplanted now themselves, sleep here; and when
Angels shall with their trumpets waken men,
And fire shall purge the world, these hence shall rise
And change their garden for a paradise.

Among the American plants that the second John brought home from Virginia was the common Spiderwort, which bears the Latin name *Tradescantia virginiana.* My two clumps are planted primarily because their purplish blue flowers with orange anthers make an effective background for my single white peonies, but also because I enjoy growing flowers whose history I know.

When, in the pause that comes to my garden after the last tulip petal has fluttered down and before the peonies open, I catch the delectable spicy fragrance of pinks, I am reminded that still another ghost walks my garden on Main Street. His was a small and only occasional part of my childhood experience, but I owe him a debt of gratitude that makes his story, however insignificant, seem worth the telling—at least to me. It always begins with his wife.

On a certain blazing hot July morning the congregation of our small Episcopal church poured out into the sunshine. There had been one of our more spectacular thunderstorms the night before, and everyone had a tale to tell. When Mrs. Gordon drifted up to Mother like a black shadow across the grass, I edged closer. Listening to Mrs. Gordon talk gave me the same eerie but delicious chill that tickled my spine when I read the more gruesome fairytales. No one ever looked so like a witch.

Whenever our church needed to raise money and put on a bazaar for that purpose, Miss Maude Mason, who lived next door to my grandmother, always supplied the fancywork table with penwipers made in the form of witches. The little figures were clad in garments made of felt in the uncompromising colors inseparable from that fabric—orange, red, yellow, blue, purple, black, and white. Between the pointed high-crowned hat and the folds of the cloak and skirt (the latter concealing some usefully absorbent material) the witch's face appeared drawn with a few pen strokes on a hickory nut. Any witch penwiper was a perfect portrait of Mrs. Gordon.

"Jane," she was saying with blistering scorn as I drew near, "has no sense at all. She got out of bed and went out on the porch to watch the lightning." I wafted an envious thought toward Jane, who was about my own age. "I," she continued, "put an old feather quilt on the floor of the closet—feathers protect you from lightning, you know. I dumped Tommy in on that and then crawled in with the baby and shut the door. It was hot as the pit, but we were safe." Her voice grew shriller, shaken with passion. "I hate thunderstorms. There are two things in this world that I really hate—thunderstorms and flowers."

Mother was probably the only woman in the group who heard this blasphemous remark with any tolerance. For ladies reared in the polite and ultra-sentimental traditions of the time, to hate flowers was almost, if not quite, sacrilegious. It was at the very least shocking. But my mother had an intelligence that transcended the fetishes of her generation. Also she was practical. It did not seem unreasonable to her that the wife of a man whose farm and whose eight children suffered from neglect while he fooled around unprofitably with flowers, should lack enthusiasm for the blossoms over which her less harassed neighbors cooed so correctly.

Child as I was, I grasped Mrs. Gordon's point, but my sympathy was for Mr. Gordon. I did not see as much of him as I did of his children but I liked him infinitely better than I did his daughter Jane, who was in my Sunday school class, or his son Sandy, who played short stop on the baseball team on which I, the only girl, covered first base.

As a matter of fact, it was chiefly in winter that I had a chance to talk to Mr. Gordon. In summer he made ineffectual efforts to farm his land, and I was busy with my own affairs. But in winter he had time to talk to a child. I must have been quite small when I came to know him.

In winter whenever mother was going to have "company" for dinner she would give me some money and send me to Mr. Gordon's, about a mile away, to buy flowers for the table. It would amuse me now to know what I carried in the pocket of my thick Peter Thompson reefer, but I no longer remember. Proabably no more than a quarter. But whatever it was it was enough. I always brought home a generous bunch of the pink or red carnations that smelled so good, or, on occasion, my favorite white ones, penciled with pink like peppermint candies.

I was enough of a country child to realize, even when I was quite small, that the Gordon place was just as down-at-the-heel as the neighbors said it was. As I turned into its lane an untidy field stretched to my left, weeds thick along the edges and in the corners. Ahead of me and to the right rose the barn, weathered grey for lack of paint. As often as not a piece of farm machinery, a plough or harrow, lay rusting beside it in the winter damp. But these things, while they impinged faintly on my consciousness, did not seem important. I felt sure that Mr.

Gordon was not intentionally a careless farmer. His heart just wasn't in the work and his mind would wander elsewhere. Mine too was already elsewhere, stretching ahead to what lay on the other side of that barn.

The south wall of the barn formed the north wall of Mr. Gordon's greenhouse. Here he had his being and here were the flowers his wife so bitterly resented.

It was a tiny place as such things go—no more than fifteen or twenty feet long and only wide enough for benches down either side of the single aisle. But to me it was magic. You stepped from crisp cold into soft, damp warmth, from a grey or white winter world into color.

Carnations took up most of the space, partly because they sold well—well, pretty well!—and thus offered an excuse for the whole outrageous expenditure of time and money. Actually, Mr. Gordon grew carnations because they were his favorite flower. He had besides, of course, potted geraniums, vivid in red and green; misty green and ecru mignonette with its exciting fragrance; begonias, pink, white, and coral-red with waxy foliage; some sort of lemon-yellow daisies, paper-white narcissus; tiny pots of lobelia of a dazzling blue; and always smoky masses of asparagus fern, without which no bouquet of the time was complete.

The knotty grey ghost of a man who presided over this fairyland was so quiet that it was hard to imagine him displaying the firmness and energy that must have been necessary to create this expression of his own individuality in the face of his ife's vociferous objections. But though Mr. Gordon was ghostlike in appearance he became humanly alive when he talked about his flowers. The child who poked slowly between the benches, peering, smelling, touching ever so gently, asking questions, was someone he could talk to. He took me into his confidence and showed me all the wonders of his small world.

Always he gave me a treasure to take home, usually just an extra flower or two, sometimes a pot with a tiny plant. But I carried away much more than the gift. While no moral maxims or exalted ideas were contributed to my education by Mr. Gordon, I always left aglow with the warmth of our friendly intercourse, the richer for some new bit of knowledge gained.

As now I look back upon what subsequently befell Mr. Gordon, it seems to have been one of those weird quirks of good luck that so rarely happen to the improvident dreamer. At the time it seemed to me entirely natural. A situation that included a witch, a ghost, and fairyland was one that properly worked out to the formula, "and they all lived happy ever after."

A couple of industrious German-Americans visited our community, on the lookout, they explained, for a site for a wholesale florist business. They were naturally referred to Mr. Gordon, who was the only person in the neighborhood possessing a greenhouse and therefore, presumably, knowledgeable about the problems involved. One thing is certain. He had not the slightest conception of flowers mass-produced for the retail trade in the nearby city. But the shrewd businessmen who talked to him saw possibilities. The neglected farm had the kind of land they wanted, plenty of room, without expensive grading, for the huge greenhouses they planned, and it was conveniently located for their market.

So far as I could make out the whole matter was settled by the florists and the two older Gordon boys without benefit of anything more from Mr. Gordon than his dazed consent, granted with the single stipulation that he was to have at least part of one greenhouse entirely for his own use. Whereupon there grew up around his bewildered person with amazing rapidity a large and profitable business.

The acres of greenhouses that flourished where the tiny one had stood had none of the latter's intimate charm, but they had their own special fascination. I spent many happy hours in them after school, wandering down one long aisle and up another, drunk in fall with the sight and smell of chrysanthemums; in winter with carnations and roses; in spring with the lilies, hyacinths, and narcissus of the Easter trade. Then, on the childhood principle of saving the best for last, I made my way to the end of the far greenhouse and Mr. Gordon. Here commerce ended and an exciting world of hitherto unknown wonders began. We talked and talked eagerly of the experiments he now had the time and the money to make. For a season or two he was interested in orchids, which would have been fabulously out of reach in the old days. One afternoon he gave me a spray of butterfly-like flowers, greenish-white with flecks of purple velvet. He had the first succulents I ever saw. Then having quenched his thirst for exotics he went back to his first love—carnations.

Mr. Gordon grew carnations of every kind and color. He would have felt scorn for the tiny pinks of my garden, even while admitting their kinship to the larger species that he loved.

Finally there came a day when Mr. Gordon showed me the result of all his work with Dianthus—his supreme triumph, a yellow carnation. This happened not long before my family moved away from that neighborhood, so I do not know whether this achievement was ever again equalled or surpassed. At the time it seemed nothing less than a miracle to us both.

It was beautiful, that very pale yellow carnation feathered

with pink. Mr. Gordon showed it to me with reverence, for was it not, under God, his own creation? By selection and patient breeding and interbreeding, by crossing and recrossing of strains, he had brought it into existence. Mr. Gordon's thin, greyish hands with their big, clumsy knuckles touched the flower delicately. His eyes, usually vague, blazed with excitement.

It is good to feel sure now, as I do, that one of Mr. Gordon's limitations proved to be a blessing to him. He was devoid of intellectual curiosity. I doubt that he ever read anything but seed catalogues and the daily paper. It is entirely safe to assume that he never so much as heard of John Parkinson's *Paradisi in sole, paradisus terrestris,* one of the earliest of English garden books, published in London in 1629. He was thus spared the knowledge that among other "delightes" in his earthly paradise Parkinson listed "the yellow or Orenge tawny Gilloflower." Parkinson saved seed from his original plant and reported that the flowers did not come true, some being a paler, some a deeper yellow than the mother plant. "Others," he continued, "are striped or spotted like a speckled carnation." Mr. Gordon's pale yellow, striped, spotted, or speckled as you please, would have been lost among its fellow "Orenge tawny Gilloflowers" in Parkinson's garden paradise. But Mr. Gordon believed that his pale yellow was unique—the first and only one ever to be seen by man. I like to think that he went to his grave with that faith unshaken.

A very pale yellow carnation feathered in pink was not at that time commercially acceptable. It would have been of no interest to the German florists, of less than no interest to the Gordon boys, on the make at last. So the total audience for Mr. Gordon's miracle was an awkward adolescent girl, peering through thick glasses at the lovely thing. In return for her interest the elderly man gave her a lifetime memory of human warmth and gentleness, of enthusiasm for a disinterested end passionately pursued, and of a dream of a world in which flowers could never be hated.

I like to think that Mr. Gordon's ghost walks in my garden when the pinks are in bloom.

15

Food in the Flower Garden

It entertains me as I walk the stone-paved paths of my garden to remember that some of my choicest treasures once went into the kitchen and thence into men's stomachs. Primroses by the peck, peony roots by the hundred dozen, lily bulbs, lupine seed, and rose petals have all at one time or another, in this part of the world or that, been considered nourishing and tasty food.

A few years ago when I was writing a series of histories of some of our garden flowers I was interested to discover that many of them had once been used by cooks in weird and wonderful ways. If I now repeat myself occasionally I trust that I may be forgiven, for here I come to the matter from a very different angle. Then the tales I told about flowers were concerned with interesting and objective facts. Now they are a part of my pleasure in gardening; and after all this book is the story of my garden on Main Street.

The first garden flower of which I have been able to find any record as an article of diet is the lupine. It appears on a list of plants grown in the kitchen garden of an Egyptian nobleman who lived about three thousand three hundred years ago. He was so important a personage that hieroglyphic records were kept of his properties and household affairs, even including such details as that lupine seeds were preserved in quantity in brine.

It may be that lupines found ancient Egypt as much to their liking as they do Vermont, for here in the northern Connecticut valley their performance is amazing. In the countryside around New York one handles lupine as if he were trying to cultivate one of the rarer forms of orchid. Yet hereabouts, whenever a seed pod by accident gets into a neighboring field, lupines rise proudly among the Indian paint brush, Queen Ann's lace, and other meadow weeds.

This I find interesting, but not nearly so much so as a fantastic coincidence in which lupine played a part. It was in Richardson Wright's *The Story of Gardening* that I read one night about lupine, growing along with chick peas and other plants, in the kitchen garden of that Egyptian nobleman. The next morning I saw on a shelf in the local supermarket a row of glass jars labelled "Lupini." And beside them, cheek by jowl so to speak, were cans of chick peas!

Of course I brought home a jar of *lupini,* and we found that, like the Egyptian product, the seeds had been preserved in brine. I had no clue as to how the Egyptians served their lupine seed but ours were obviously intended to be eaten just as they came from the jars. So we tried them out that evening with cocktails, and I regret to report that in spite of the brine their flavor was deplorably reminiscent of cheap perfume.

Between that American cocktail party and the meals served to the Egyptian prince stretches a long culinary history of lupines highlighted by some of the odd ways in which they were served as food.

There was, for instance, the Greek artist Protogenes, who flourished toward the end of the fourth century B.C. He was commissioned to paint a hunting scene, and it took him seven years to do it. Lupine seeds were not only an acceptable and nourishing food but they were reputed to brighten the mind and quicken the imagination. So Protogenes, in the interest of art, lived for all those seven years on lupine seed and water. Unfortunately the picture has not survived to give us any indication how valuable lupines are to artistic inspiration.

Two thousand years later German scientists, working to develop ersatz foods during World War One, came up with some extraordinary uses for lupine. To display their achievement, a group of botanists were invited to a banquet in Hamburg. The table was spread with a cloth made of lupine fiber. Lupine soup was the first item on the menu. Lupine "beefsteak" followed, cooked with lupine oil and flavored with lupine extract. The bread contained lupine meal and was spread with margarine made from lupine oil. There was also a lupine "cheese," lupine "coffee," and finally a lupine "liqueur." The bare facts give us no clue as to how much the botanists enjoyed this repast.

A huge volume could be compiled of rose receipts, ancient and modern. As a matter of fact a small volume containing some of these lies on my desk as I write—*Rose Receipts* by Jean Gordon, published in Woodstock, Vermont, in 1958. Here, taken at random, are a few of the ways in which roses have found and still sometimes find a place in the kitchen—rose custard, rose-petal pudding, pistachio and rose ice cream, rose-petal preserves and rose-apple jelly. A receipt is also included for rose butter, an old and popular English delicacy with which sandwiches may be spread for the traditional afternoon tea. Sweet butter, surrounded and covered with rose petals, is put in a tightly covered container over night; by morning the butter will have absorbed the perfume and flavor of roses.

Of all the thousands of receipts using rose petals, probably the largest number deal with the making of rose water. Long after vanilla had reached European kitchens from Mexico it remained a rare and expensive luxury. Rose water continued to serve as the most popular flavoring at the cook's disposal until well into the nineteenth century, partly, it is safe to assume, from habit but also because it was much less expensive than was the exotic novelty from the tropics.

More expensive than rose water, but for all that widely and lavishly used, was saffron. When crocuses bring spring to my garden and the flowers open to show the gaudy red-orange of their pistils and stamens I always think of their near relative *Crocus sativus*. This looks very like one of my gold crocuses, but it blooms in the fall and yields the fragrant coloring matter which is still sometimes used to brighten and flavor Spanish chicken and rice dishes. In earlier times and especially during the Middle Ages, saffron was par excellence the flavor of flavors. In addition to imparting a subtle tang to food it enlivened with its brilliant color any dish in which it was used. As one turns the pages of medieval cookbooks—which are of course transcriptions from old rolls—it is soon apparent that saffron was used in anything and everything from soup to dessert. You had to have saffron to "Make a Fayre Garbage"—chicken giblets and feet stewed in broth. Saffron colored and flavored "Smal Byrdys Y-Stwyded." Saffron also supplied a cheerful golden tint to the pastry shells known as "Smal Cofynes," which were filled with raw egg yolks, dotted with "gobytys" of marrow and then covered with the coffin lids before baking. But of all these fascinating medieval dishes my favorite is "Cokyntryce."

Cokyntryce was definitely designed for high days and holidays, since it was far too difficult to make to toss off for a family meal. To make Cokyntryce you take a capon and "smyte hem in the waste across." You then also bisect a "Pigge" in the same manner, after which you "sewe the fore party of the Capoun to the After parti of the Pigge" and then sew "the fore parte of the Pigge to the hynder party of the Capoun." The two monsters so constructed are roasted on a spit and, when done, "gylded" with the yolks of eggs, with ginger, and with saffron.

The hot bright color at the heart of my crocuses in a chilly New England garden throws a shaft of light all the way back to those gilded beasts roasting before an open fire in a smoky, sooty, castle kitchen in England five hundred years ago.

Primroses provide the Englishman a link to the past far better than they can any American. Primroses, cowslips, and oxlips are all wild flowers in the British Isles, as familiar and common as dandelions. And like dandelions they were used without stint. A receipt dated about two hundred years ago begins with the startling injunction, "Take a peck of primroses." As the instructions continue we are reminded of a lavishness still known to our grandmothers but lost now to the modern world. In those days there was no skimping of time, labor, or materials. That peck of primrose flowers had to be washed and chopped fine. To these were added half a pound of Naples Biscuit (ladyfingers to us) grated, three pints of cream, sixteen eggs, and a little rose water. "Sweeten to your Palate." The custard so made could be baked or, if you wanted to make tarts, it could be poured into pastry shells.

An American gardener shudders at that curt direction—"Take a peck of primroses." On this side of the Atlantic primroses are exotics, far too delicate and precious to be thought of as food. Yet their history in English kitchens is so voluminous that if one reads many of the old receipts one comes gradually to accept primroses as natural ingredients in numerous puddings, pies, and tarts. They are still, I believe, sometimes so used in England.

Roses, saffron, and primroses all have long histories in the kitchen, reaching back steadily from our own time, or very near it, to the remote past. Most other flowers that have turned up on menus have, however, done so spasmodically—now in this period, now in that; sometimes in one part of the world, sometimes in another. For this reason a gardener's interest in flowers as food tends to focus, among the many choices, on those that fall in with his personal predilections. I, for example, was far more interested in the single reference I found to columbines than I was in numerous Oriental receipts in which lily bulbs were used. A gardener more knowledgeable about the Far East than I would probably think my columbine trivial, while he would revel in reading about all the ways in which lily bulbs have been cooked and eaten in Asia.

My single reference to columbines in the kitchen carried me happily back into a familiar world—so happily that it sent me scurrying to old records in order to get all the details about the scene in which columbines—blue English columbines—played a modest part.

"Gellie coloured with columbine flowers" was an item on the menu of the banquet Henry V gave to celebrate the coronation of his "little French fleur-de-lis" whom he married six years after his great victory at Agincourt. Like Shakespeare before me—though hardly with such spectacular results—I went to Holinshed to find out what I could about that banquet. I was rewarded with a detailed description.

The King and Queen sat side by side at tables on a dais, while on the floor below stretched the long board around which were gathered the nobility and gentry of their court. Holinshed does not supply the color of that scene, but it blazes for us on manuscripts of the time—scarlet and gold, ultramarine and silver, violet, lemon yellow, and Lincoln green. A more somber figure, the earl marshal, clad in armor and astride a great courser, rode round and round the great hall keeping order. His wife the "countess marshall" and the Countess of Kent sat under the Queen's table.

Under the Queen's table! But so said Holinshed, and I was agog to discover the explanation of this peculiar aspect of fifteenth century etiquette. When none of the books I consulted on English manners and customs provided me with one, I went to the reference department of the New York Public Library. And as always I went not in vain. Someone patiently worked on that tedious bit of research that had baffled me and finally came up with chapter and verse to prove that the difficulty involved was not one of etiquette but of semantics.

The two ladies had occupied a small table on the main floor below the dais, thus *below* the Queen's table, not *under* it.

Even if that banquet, which took place in England nearly five and a half centuries ago, seems far removed from my garden on Main Street, there is a connection between the two, tenuous, but very real to me.

The imagination of today's young generation is being fired by the science fiction that is coming true before their eyes on TV. Their fathers sat breathless when the radio sang out "Hi-Yo Silver!" and tales of the Wild West set ten-year-old pulses racing. My generation turned the pages of books but with hardly less excitement. *When Knighthood Was in Flower,* as a popular play of the time described it, was the period that provided us with adventures, glamor, and thrills. King Arthur and his knights of the Round Table, Robin Hood, Little John, and Will Scarlet, Ivanhoe, Otto of the Silver Hand, Myles Falworth in *Men of Iron,* to name only a few, were familiar, beloved, and heroic figures to us. Like the banqueters at Henry's feast they too walked or rode, when not clad in impressive metallic battle dress, in the scarlet and gold, violet and silver, ultramarine and lemon yellow, Lincoln green and russet brown of their time.

Those of us who became enamored of these colorful figures later turned to more solid history of early England. Shakespeare provided vivid personal portraits which, while not always strictly accurate from the historian's point of view, added immeasurably to our sense of the living past. Thus it is just as natural for me to be intrigued by a banquet given by the last of the great medieval knights as it is for me to be captivated by columbines swinging on their wiry stems in my garden. When, as in this case, I can find a connection between feast and flower, I am enchanted.

Peonies, however, played a far more important role in the medieval cuisine than columbines did. Judging by the banquets on whose menus "peonys," "pyonys," "pionys," and other variations of the name appeared, peony roots were considered, quite literally, as food fit for a king. The hundred-dozen peony roots which the Duke of Lancaster ordered for the feast he gave Richard II must have cost a fabulous sum. For this was no common food for common men, since peonies are not native to England, to be gathered in quantity in any field or copse.

Yet peony roots did not appear at that banquet that Henry gave for his newly crowned queen when jelly, colored with columbine flowers, was served. Perhaps the king did not care for the royal peony dish. He could have tasted it, as a child of twelve, when peony roots were served "rosted" at his father's coronation banquet in 1399 and again, five years later, at the feast Henry IV gave to celebrate his second marriage. By that time the little boy would have become the madcap Prince Hal, a problem adolescent, roystering around the streets of London with Falstaff and his crew.

If two Henrys, father and son, not to mention Richard II and most of the great knights of the time could eat peony roots, I saw no reason why two modern Americans should not try them. Not, I hasten to add, the roots of my single white ones, but some well established, old plants that were about to be discarded. I roasted some of their roots along with a loin of pork. My husband and I are now quite satisfied that we know why peony roots as a special delicacy did not survive the fifteenth century.

Other flowers, of course, found their way into the kitchen though in less spectacular ways. Pinks were used often in the hope that their clovelike fragrance might serve as a cheap substitute for the expensive luxury from the Far East. Sops in wine they were called in Shakespeare's time. Calendula petals, fresh or dried, were long considered an indispensable addition to broths and stews.

The flowers in my garden seem somehow gayer and more interesting because of their varied activities in the kitchen. I enjoy the picturesque stories about their adventures there, but I am well content to ignore their value as food or flavoring and cherish my flowers only as garden ornaments.

Across
the Fence

The contacts that have come to me across the fence have, by and large, been pleasant ones—friendly, amusing, or interesting. All the village goes by just a few feet from where I work and, while I continue to envy my neighbors who have back-yard gardens, I am not ungrateful for the compensations that gardening in public has brought me.

Not all my contacts across the fence, however, have generated sweetness and light. There are times when I must count over those compensations as one deliberately counts one's blessings in order to lighten the burden of the moment. Robert Frost contends that good fences make good neighbors, so perhaps the very flimsiness of my picket fence explains why some of my contacts across it have failed to produce this pleasing result.

Failure was especially marked in the case of the kittens. A woman who lived near us had three or four half-grown ones who infested my garden. She and I discussed the matter across the fence, and I pointed out that the kittens were more than welcome to the whole of our big back yard if only she would let them out from the basement of her house instead of at street level. Grudgingly she agreed. But the nuisance of shepherding those small demons downstairs proved too much for her. It was easier to open the front door. The result was that I spent the first part of every morning that spring chasing kittens with a long switch, proof positive in my neighbor's eyes that I was lying when I claimed that I liked cats. The switch was a mere prop, designed to strike nothing but terror. And, if they could speak, the black and white, yellow and tabby ghosts of Madame Queen and Talcum, Lemuel and Scutty would establish the validity of my claim.

Other results of these feline forays were to haunt me throughout the rest of the season. The worst was the loss of a whole stand of Henryi lilies. When a fine array of their young shoots was six or eight inches high, the kittens decided to settle some fratricidal dispute on that exact spot. All the shoots were broken, and I mourned the destruction of what had, the year before, been a spectacular display. Nor did I mourn in silence. As a result, what had started as an effort to resolve a difficulty in a neighborly spirit across the fence, degenerated into unneighborly frigidity. The only reason ours is a catless household is that neither my husband nor I can face becoming fond of a small animal that could be so easily destroyed before our eyes in the traffic that swishes past our front door from morning until night.

The kittens may stand—no, they were never still long enough to stand—but we may take their hectic activity as symbolic of the occasional minor irritations that came my way as I gardened in public. Few were as disturbing as the kittens. For, as I trust I shall be able to show, I have been very lucky in that most of my contacts across the fence have been pleasurable ones.

One fine May morning a unique and charming picture was presented to me. The president of our local garden club stopped by. Her mother had driven over with her, but since the old lady is not quite as spry as she used to be, she stayed on the sidewalk near the car while we two went into the garden. We were so absorbed in matters of mutual interest that I did not hear a man approaching until a rich Irish brogue boomed out, "The top of the morning to you, Mrs. Conlin. And how do you find yourself this foin day?"

"Well enough to dance a jig with you, Michael O'Harrigan," replied the old lady saucily—and began. The man swept off his hat and squared off opposite her. It only lasted a moment. The two old figures moved jerkily like wooden dolls whose wired joints have grown rusty but, all the same, for no more than a breath of time, there it was: an authentic Irish jig danced on the main street of a Vermont village. Mrs. Conlin, I knew, had celebrated her ninety-fourth birthday only a week before.

Quantities of children go by my garden on their way to and from school in the spring and fall. Few stop or comment, but I enjoy the cheerful "Hi" that most of them toss me across the fence as they go by.

Those who do stop often puzzle me. These are country children born and bred, yet they often do not know the names of the commonest garden flowers.

"What's that?" a little girl asked me one day, pointing to some nasturtiums. I told her, and as I handed her a flower and a couple of the leaves, I asked her if she didn't like the taste of the stems. She put one to her lips dubiously as I went back to work, wondering what sort of country child this could be who did not know the nip and bite of that pungent flavor on the tongue.

The goldfish in the little pool interested some of the boys and we occasionally had learned discussions about tadpoles, fish, and fishing. They are very knowledgeable about fishing in this trout-stream country.

By and large, however, the children hurry by, too busy with their own concerns—as they should be—to bother about mine. But one day a little boy who had come along alone lingered so long that I looked up and smiled.

"It's pretty," he said shyly and scuttled away.

I probably have the general juvenile indifference to thank for the fact that my garden has been so rarely violated. Once some imp tossed a half-eaten ice-cream cone into the pool, and I clear out chewing-gum wrappers as regularly as I do weeds, but in general the children have not been vandals.

There was, though, a day when I did mourn the loss of half a dozen fine lily-flowered white tulips that had been growing in front of the house. To a neighbor who came by on her way to work I voiced by indignation. She was unsympathetic.

"The little darling probably wanted to take them home to his mother," she said blandly.

My answer was prompt and explicit.

"Look out in the street," I told her. "That's how your little darling took them home to mother."

The flowers, broken off with only an inch or two of stem, lay scattered over U.S. Highway 5—which is Main Street in our town—some of them already crushed by passing cars.

The Methodist minister, who lives a few doors to the south

of us, is one of my most frequent across-the-fence visitors. He enjoys my garden and can talk about it intelligently, although his wife is the gardener in their family. He has actually used my lilies and Christmas roses in sermons, or so I am informed by the village grapevine, since I do not attend his church.

One summer afternoon he appeared on my doorstep with a small potted plant in his hand, a charming little thing he called a rainbow ivy. Its toothed and pointed leaves were edged with a deep band of cream color and underneath were a very warm reddish lavender.

"My wife and I have enjoyed your garden so much," he told me, "that when we saw this at a nursery yesterday we decided to get it for you."

I was delighted not only to receive such flattering appreciation but also to find that the minister was as tickled at my most outlandish horticultural joke as I was myself.

It was winter and the last flowers on two magnificent amaryllis in my front living-room windows were beginning to curl at the edges. I hated to have Love's Desire fold up on me, but the end was obviously near. I donned galoshes, a heavy coat, cap, and gloves and cut both scapes, each holding two flowers. These I carried outdoors. To the right and left of our entrance path were mammoth mounds of snow, thrown up there by the boy who shovels for us. I stuck a scape into the top of each mound, and, since it was twenty below zero, the flowers froze almost instantly to a brittle, porcelain-like texture. They remained in place for several days, flaunting pink defiance to the white winter world, to the considerable amusement of my neighbors and especially of my clerical friend.

A great many other neighbors pass along the sidewalk and stop to admire my garden. To say that I enjoy this is understatement: like most gardeners I am a sucker for flattery. A personal remark or even a kind word about my writing tends to embarrass me, but when it comes to the garden flattery can be laid on with a shovel.

Some of my visitors are gardeners themselves, who often stop to discuss garden matters or exchange experiences. There is one village woman who is particularly sympathetic to me because she has become so interested in gardening that she has studied some botany and read widely. Botanical names trip as easily from her tongue as from that of an expert, but she is without pretension and gives commoner plants their ordinary names. A columbine is always a columbine to her, although she knows quite well that it is also an aquilegia. But such technical knowledge is rare. Many a local gardener who can grow far handsomer cosmos or chrysanthemums than I is entirely unaware that the two plants belong to the same family.

Some of my visitors bring me plants; while I should like to name them all in gratitude I shall mention as a sample only the New Hampshireman who brought me the generous collection of coral-bells. These now fringe the path from the house to the garden, and I think of him gratefully as the tall stems wave whenever I pass.

One afternoon a pretty Polish-American girl walking with a stout elderly woman passed and then came back. She said that her mother would like to know the name of the feathery little shrub growing on either side of our entrance path but could not speak enough English to ask me herself. I told the girl that it was southernwood and was only too glad to be able to scrabble around and find a few rooted stems for her. I trust that sturdy plants are now flourishing in Little Warsaw, as their section of the village is called.

One morning an out-of-town car slowed as it passed the garden and parked farther along the street. Three charming women about my age walked back to talk to me across the fence. One was from Connecticut, the other two from Massachusetts, total strangers to me, but we all talked happily and volubly about a mutual interest.

Another day a woman strolling on the sidewalk paused outside the fence to talk to me. She was from Iowa, she told me, and had asked her husband to stop the car so she might stretch her legs. She admired my garden and was soon telling me about the one she tended at home. She was enchanted by the pool because she remembered well the iron sink in her grandmother's kitchen. When I demonstrated its mechanism she was so interested and pleased that I have since wondered if that Iowa garden ever acquired a pool like mine.

Friends, of course, come often. Since some of these are gardeners, with them I plunge happily into the technicalities of the vocation we share. With others, talk tends to follow more personal lines—the visiting grandchildren, the latest local news.

There was one friend who used to drive over from New Hampshire every morning to get his paper and would often stop to greet me. He would stand chuckling on the sidewalk while I scrambled hastily from my knees, threw first one, then the other jean-clad leg over the fence to join him. He would be rolling a cigarette by the time I reached him, Bull Durham spilling generously over his vest and down onto the concrete pavement. "Tobacco Road," his sister called him.

Our talk was of the small doings of our lives: the trip in the car yesterday, the beauty of the delphinium in his wife's garden, the friends expected for the weekend. And all the while he would catch me up on every incorrect use of "will" or "shall," "would" or "should," for he was enlivening his old age by a crusade to have those maltreated parts of speech used with classic precision.

His own English was perfect and his talk—well, perhaps my son has described it best. He had spent a good part of a day with this old friend of ours, having been asked over for lunch and a game of chess. Kirk, still an undergraduate at the time, had accepted this invitation with enthusiasm untroubled by the fact that his prospective host was nearly sixty years his senior.

"Did you have a good time?" I asked automatically when Kirk came home.

"Sure," he replied just as automatically. Then he added, pleasure still vibrant in his voice, "It was great fun. Mr. A. has something I thought had died with the eighteenth century—wit."

Behind that wit, behind the gay ephemeral charm, lay the rich texture of Jack's mind. He knew Shakespeare not as a scholar but as a lover and could recite long speeches and whole scenes by heart. He was a retired architect, learned in his profession and sensitive to art in every form.

He shared with my husband and me a special bond of sympathy. This we discovered early in our acquaintance at a cocktail party when some discussion about politics arose. Knowing that sooner or later my own political iniquities must come to light in this rock-ribbed Republican milieu, I admitted to pride in the fact that I had voted for Roosevelt all four times. An icy silence greeted my remark. Then at my elbow I heard a voice saying thoughtfully, "Four times? No. Three. I voted for Norman Thomas the first time."

A couple of years after the death of this friend I started to speak of him to an eminent scholar whose friendship we had shared. "Don't" he interrupted quickly. "Please, Buckie, don't.

I can't bear to talk about Jack, I miss him so dreadfully."

Among the people with whom I talk across the fence are some I call regulars, not only because they go by every day, but because they go by at the same time every day.

One summer there was an old woman whose only exercise was her daily trip to buy groceries. She always paused to greet me, admire the garden, and have a little chat. Her special interest was the pool. There were goldfish in it, then, and it was on these that she concentrated her concern. She would fold her hands across her stomach, gaze down at the water and say, almost with a smack of the lips, "Pussy will get them." Then, with the ghoulish delight in catastrophy of the emotionally starved, she would repeat hopefully, "Pussy will get them."

Another year there was a very old man who crept by every morning.

"Still at it," he remarked the first time I looked up and saw him. I made some sort of reply. He did not answer. Perhaps he was deaf.

Every morning for the rest of the summer he would stop at the fence. "Still at it," he would say and then shuffle along, apparently content that I had looked up and smiled. This tenuous human contact seemed to give him pleasure.

Many a time since then I have heard the echo of that wavering old voice in my ears as I drop to my knees, fork in hand, weeding basket beside me. "Still at it."

Index

Index